Hoopla in Harlem!

The Renaissance of African American Art and Culture

D1606158

A Rhetorical Criticism of Artists as Social Activists During the 1920s and 1930s; Engaging the Philosophical Discourse of Kenneth Burke

Lan...mouth, UK

Copyright © 2009 by
University Press of America,® Inc.
4501 Forbes Boulevard
Suite 200
Lanham, Maryland 20706
UPA Acquisitions Department (301) 459-3366

Estover Road
Plymouth PL6 7PY
United Kingdom

Library of Congress Control Number: 2009922300
ISBN: 978-0-7618-4570-6 (paperback : alk. paper)
eISBN: 978-0-7618-4571-3

⊖™ The paper used in this publication meets the minimum
requirements of American National Standard for Information
Sciences—Permanence of Paper for Printed Library Materials,
ANSI Z39.48—1984

CONTENTS

PREFACE

Harlem glittered as one on the world's most vivid entertainment centers during the 1920's and 30's. Nightlife revolved around The Cotton Club, Smalls Paradise and The Savoy Ballroom; featuring floor shows headlining glamorous African American women and whiskey unavailable in downtown Greenwich Village clubs. African American Artists during the Harlem Renaissance were Social Activists, making a significant contribution to black culture and aesthetics. Creating the notions of Black Identity, Black Consciousness and Black Pride Sustained these Artists as Activists in the face of adversity and placed "The New Negro" on the global artistic scene. Dr. Alain Locke wrote the manifesto for "The New Negro" movement and W.E.B. DuBois was the harbinder to lead a cadre of African American Artists to Harlem, their creative promised land. From the world of literature, Jessie Fauset and James Weldon Johnson; From the world of dance and music, Katherine Dunham and Marian Anderson; From the world of theatre and film, Paul Robeson and Oscar Micheaux. This dissertation examines these Artists as Activists and their works as symbols of social protest, engaging the philosophical discourse of Kenneth Burke.

1
INTRODUCTION

The dawn of the twentieth century in the United States brought about increasing racial conflict and great moral controversy. W.E.B. DuBois argued that the "color line" would be the biggest social and moral issue for America during the twentieth century. African Americans demanded simple freedom, liberation and equal treatment. Instead, they received lynching and mob violence. The nonviolent marches and boycotts during the Harlem Renaissance in the 1920s and 1930s signaled the beginning of African American protests against racial injustices.

Out of the ashes and fire of lynched African Americans rose a great "Phoenix" of social protest, William Edward Burghardt (W.E.B.) DuBois. During the Harlem Renaissance the sociological interpretation of race took precedence and became firmly entrenched in the American mindset. Race is linked to racism and to the idea of white versus black. This sociological context of race is evident from the moment the first slave touched American soil. Race in this context is rooted in racialism, the belief that racial differences result from black inferiority and white superiority.

Blacks have not simply been treated unfairly; they have been subjected first to decades of slavery, then to decades of second-class citizenship, massive legalized discrimination, economic persecution, educational deprivation and cultural stigmatization; they have been killed, beaten, raped, bought, sold, excluded, exploited, shamed, and scorned. Yet they have become increasingly successful against the odds.

The rhetoric of oppression, constructed by mainstream society during the 1920s continues to negate the humanity of African Americans. The rhetoric of oppression is crafted to maintain eurocentric economic hegemony. Hence, with urgency, the rhetoric of protest is crafted to dismantle the constructed, stereotypical, ethnocentric myths. Because of the peculiar institution of slavery, African American rhetors created protest rhetoric to respond to oppression. Crafting the rhetoric of resistance to respond to the rhetoric of oppression; gives credence to an oratorical and elocutionary movement of African American protest rhetoric during the Harlem Renaissance of the 1920s and 1930s.

African American language is rooted in an oral tradition and because it has grown out of a sociopolitical and cultural climate unlike that experienced by any other ethnic group. As Hoyt Fuller states, "African American Culture is the aesthetic record of our sojourn here, reflecting as all literatures do, the core concerns of a people."[1]

The language used in African American culture reflects the African American experience and therefore, is rhetorically unique. One reason for this uniqueness is that as the myriads of African tribes with different dialects met on American soil, they had to find a common language communicating their needs and fears. As their rebellious attitude grew, the newcomers found it expedient to devise a communication system that would be meaningful to other African Americans but not understood by whites. Hence, it was necessary to take the "master's" language and to manipulate it to suit their own needs."[2]   Blacks often changed the meaning of a word completely to mask their true feelings.

This alteration of language by slaves has persisted through the ages, and even today this double talk/ signification persists. African American speech, is used as a defense mechanism and as an articulation of the revolutionary spirit of protest. Grace Holt contends that, *"African Americans' use of metaphor is an outgrowth of their attempt at survival dealing with racist White America."*[3]

Accordingly, it was natural that this rhetorical strategy of changing the spoken word would find its way into written language, especially African American protest literature. Thus, it is this kind of linguistic strategy—the altering of language—as well as classical rhetorical devices that I will examine in the protest rhetoric of DuBois and the Artists of the Harlem Renaissance.

Richard Barksdale and Kenneth Kinnamon make a definitive statement about the themes of African American culture from 1915 to 1945. The dominant theme, they claim, "was racial affirmation from 1915-1930, and from 1930-45 the dominant theme was radical racial protest."[4]   The first definition given in *Webster's New World Dictionary* for both words "protest" and "affirm" is basically the same: to state positively, to affirm solemnly (for "protest") and to declare firmly (for "affirm"). Then the second definition for "protest" is to make objections; to speak strongly against. The basic meaning in the "public domain" is that protest rhetoric is that rhetoric which makes objections to the status quo. Furthermore, the division between protest and affirmation is weakened more if one considers the fact that if a person has to affirm his existence, his culture, then he is protesting to the person who wishes to deny his existence, or culture *"when a person is denied that which is his, he objects strongly by declaring firmly,"* according to Ralph Ellison, *"I am what I am."*[5] Although the denotative meanings are similar, a split is created between the connotative interpretation of the words "protest" and "affirmation". Larry Neal clarifies the definition this way. *"Now any Black man who adheres to the white aesthetic, and who directs his work toward a white audience is protesting."*[6]

According to Don L. Lee (A.K.A.) Haki Madhubuti, an African American civil rights rhetor attempts to raise the level of consciousness among African Americans. Madhubuti describes protest as rhetoric which is a reaction to persons or events and often necessary to motivate and move people. As African American rhetors rejected Western aesthetics and labels and any other Western values that stood in the way of their affirmation of Blackness, *"they set up their own aesthetics, commonly referred to as the Black Arts Movement."*[7] The proponents of this movement were also concerned with raising the consciousness of African Americans and helping them to affirm their Blackness as well as their manhood. In writing this kind of language, the rhetors knew that they had to use the language, symbols, ideology, and national heroes of the people for whom and about whom they wrote. These rhetors knew, but did not care, that to assert their Blackness was to be considered "militant," "dangerous," "subversive," and "revolutionary."[8] African American rhetors protests were based upon the inequities of the American experience, the so-called American Dream, a dream for whom? For as Grace Holt declares: *"An affirmation of self, raises levels of commitment to resistance..."*[9]

The obvious necessity for this dissertation research is that African American Culture has been silent, hidden, marginalized and oppressed. Because African American men are an endangered species; teenage pregnancy looming large; an attack on affirmative action; increasing intolerance of minority issues by racist republicanism, there is truly a great need for this dissertation. This study is important because it is a pedagogical tool, which can be used in the teaching and retention of African American students, so they can learn, know and love their rich African American cultural heritage. Also, this study is necessary because it can be an educational tool for white students, as they can come to know and understand African American culture, thus making a strong commitment to multiculturalism and diversity.

This dissertation is a contribution to knowledge because it gives legitimacy to African American Voices raised in Protest. One hardly need mention that the rhetoric of African American Artists is obscured, marginalized and silenced as "Other". The rhetoric of African American Artists has been even less studied in the American Academy, an institution that has traditionally been consumed with the study of the so-called great (usually dead) white male. Such neglect is all the more shameful given the African American history of powerful oratory. If we but listen, these are voices that have echoed down through our history even to the present day.

The foundations of this movement were laid in the social and political thought of the early 20th century. The African American political leader W.E.B. DuBois, editor of the influential magazine *The Crisis*, rejected the notion that African Americans could achieve social equality by emulating white ideals, and he worked for the renewal of African American racial pride through an emphasis on an African cultural heritage. The Artists as Activists during the Harlem Renaissance had in common the experience of their race, and their artistic work formed the first substantial body of art to deal with African American life from an African American perspective. These Artists as Activists sought the challenge of a freedom-seeking African American identity, social consciousness and political activism; which is increasingly depicted through their vivid artistic accomplishments. In essence, the Harlem Renaissance was a social movement, a series of organized activities working toward a common objective; it was an organized effort to promote or attain an end, Black Identity, Black Consciousness, Black Pride, Black Culture via Black Protest Rhetoric.

The Artists as Activists during the Harlem Renaissance examined themselves and looked at their unique and distinguishing qualities. Despite the trials and tribulations, the African American community has developed a number of distinctive cultural features that African Americans increasingly look upon with pride. Many of these features reflect the influence of cultural traditions that originated in Africa; others reflect the uniqueness of the African American in the United States. The unique features of African American culture are most noticeable in music, art, dance, literature, theatre, and film. No published scholarship argues that the Harlem Cultural Revolution was the single most important Social Movement in the African American community before the Black Power Sixties. I will examine in this study how the Harlem Renaissance became a testament to the making of a critical, creative Social Movement that pushed African American Artistic endeavors to the forefront of the American and international stage.

As this dissertation is to fulfill the requirement in the program of Interdisciplinary Humanities, the thrust of this dissertation is increasingly interdisciplinary. No one person, idea or situation created the articulations of Black Protest Rhetoric during the Harlem Renaissance. I have chosen the following group of African Americans for their contributions to African American culture and their significant contributions in establishing a strong Black Identity, Black Consciousness and Black Pride via Black Protest Rhetoric. In the field of Interdisciplinary Humanities, From the World of Literature: Jessie Fauset, James Weldon Johnson; From the World of Dance: Katherine Dunham; From the World of Music: Marian Anderson; From the World of Theatre: Paul Robeson; From the World of Film: Oscar Micheaux. Each of these African American Artists made significant contributions not only to Black Culture and Aesthetics, also to the international artistic community. Not only are these African Americans Artists but Activists as well, taking Black Culture from the racist American society to the international capitals of the world; at a time when African Americans were treated as second-class citizens.

Thus, I contend I am making a significant contribution to knowledge, by examining these Harlem Renaissance Artists as Activists and using this research as a pedagogical tool to educate students. However, I will demonstrate how the Harlem Renaissance was a necessary precursor to the 60s rhetoric.

THE PERIOD: HARLEM RENAISSANCE DURING THE 20S AND 30S

By the end of World War I, African Americans recognized their need for racial identity, consciousness, and pride in order to define their own standards of beauty. Orator Marcus Garvey (1887-1940) fostered Black Nationalism by traveling through the country to promote unity among African-Americans. His popular Universal Negro Improvement Association grew to international scope. His enthusiasm for ethnic pride is conveyed in the enduring phrase he originated, "Black is Beautiful."

Harlem glittered as one of New York's entertainment centers in the 1920s. Nightlife revolved around the Cotton Club and the Apollo Theatre, where Blacks and Whites watched floor shows headlining glamorous African American showgirls and drank whiskey unavailable in downtown clubs. Something like the concept of African American culture, identity and aesthetics had to be on James Weldon Johnson's mind, for instance, when he wrote in the preface of his 1922 anthology, *The Book of American Negro Poetry*, calling for racial uplift through the creation of art: "No people that has produced great literature and art has ever been looked upon by the world as distinctly inferior."[10]

Put another way, the Harlem Renaissance, gave us the cultural paradigms for seeing African Americans in a different light. African American expression in relation to modern American popular culture, it might be time to recast our concerns, deconstruct mythologies of American popular culture and high cultures and give African American expression its long overdue position; "as literary, visual, and provocative performing artistic gems."[11]

This means that by 1922 when, according to most scholars, the Harlem Renaissance had already begun, there was already a distinctive artform associated with Harlem, a school of art, if you will. Most people think of the Harlem Renaissance through literature, however, music, dance, theatre, film-all of the fine and performing arts added to the relevance of the Harlem Renaissance as a movement of social protest.

African American musicians created a concept of protest by forming their own bands, as no White bands wanted to hire Black musicians such as Duke Ellington, and Fletcher Henderson. Ellington and Henderson extended the tradition of the urban Black Big Bands, established back in 1910 by James Reese Europe, (with his 125-piece Carnegie Hall band and his radical formation of New York black musicians) into the Clef Club. *"Had not Europe been murdered by a disgruntled drummer in 1919, he would have been at least as influential a band leader as Ellington and Henderson."[12]* One reason that Europe is not more noted is because his music was produced before the days of rampant recording and radio and thus much of it is unpreserved, although Europe was commemorated in the 1943 black musical film, *Stormy Weather*.

It is increasingly relevant to Black Protest to understand that Blacks during the Harlem Renaissance were starting to create their own notions of Art. Blacks were not looking to white themes to produce art but to African themes.

It was during the twenties that a great deal of interest in creating symphonic, composed jazz was expressed by Blacks. James P. Johnson and his student, Fats Waller, gave such a concert in the late 1920s. If jazz was to become a more formally composed, arranged, "symphonic" music, then it goes without saying that the piano would be the central instrument to effect such a transition.

The writers of the Harlem Renaissance were an extremely mobile crew, who felt joined, not estranged, by their wanderings, because they were part of the great migration of African American people to the urban Northeast around World War I. Collectively they developed a vision of an urban home that was at once an organic place, a birthright community, and a cultural aspiration. In all three of these dimensions, the vitality of Harlem reached out even across continents joined in oppression. And Harlem, New York, their capital city within a city, was the center. Whether or not they happened to be living there at any particular time, the Harlem Renaissance Artists regarded Harlem as their primary, symbolic home. Thus, their Harlem focused an exemplary attempt to make a home for modern urban transients. Their lives and works tried Harlem's strengths as well as its limitations as home, place and community. Great aspirations gave rise to a distinct African American identity and consciousness in a place called Harlem.

Nearly all the Harlem Renaissance writers were urban. Even those who were raised in small towns came to Harlem via other cities - Northerner W.E.B. DuBois from the faculty of Atlanta University, Southerner Zora Neale Hurston from service as a manicurist in Washington, D.C., Westerner Wallace Thurman from the post office in Los Angeles. Young Langston Hughes arrived from Cleveland, Nella Larsen from Chicago, Rudolph Fisher from Washington, DC, Dorothy West from Boston; and before them, James Weldon Johnson came from Jacksonville, Walter White from Atlanta, Jessie Fauset from Philadelphia, and Claude McKay from Kingston, Jamaica. They were from cities and on the move. In fact, the best publicized "New Negro" leaders of the Harlem Renaissance were more often away than in residence during the 1920s: Claude McKay took off in 1922 for a twelve-year vagabondage through major cities of Europe and Africa; loyal Langston Hughes just kept coming back from sea or college for Harlem weekends, vacations, and special occasions; and Countee Cullen, the only leader of the Harlem Renaissance raised in New York City, was away over half the time at Harvard, then in Paris, escaping the racism and segregation in America. So many Renaissance Harlemites flocked to Paris because of racism and segregation that Alain Locke once called it a "transplanted Harlem." Even for the senior writers who were also political organizers, editors, and its most stable residents, Harlem was a rather brief hegira.

The Artists' urban wanderlust, however, only increased their identification with Harlem as the hub of a dynamic world. "Harlem was the goal of many African American migrants in the 1910s and 1920s, collecting over 200,000 Black residents by 1930."[13] Because the city's economy was service-oriented rather than industrial, Manhattan did not draw the predominantly rural, unskilled

Blacks who migrated to other Northern cities. And they came because Harlem was the symbolic center of African America, generally -- the Negro Capital or Mecca or Promised Land, as it was variously dubbed.

Artists lived as Activists at the time of the Harlem Renaissance; during the 1920s and 30s notable productions of African American literature, music, dance, theatre and film took place, and ergo, race consciousness increased. The Artists as Activists during the Harlem Renaissance created a reinforcement of ethnic identity among urban African Americans. The advocacy of social change gave rise to the building of a Black National Consciousness. Black Identity, Black Consciousness, Black Pride, gives credence to the critical perspective that the Harlem Renaissance created a Social Movement of Self-Determination for African Americans, long before Dr. Martin Luther King Jr. and the Civil Rights Movement of the 1960s. The Harlem Renaissance as a social movement wrought dramatic change and laid the foundation for Dr. Martin Luther King Jr. and the Civil Rights Movement of the 1960s.

The famous historian Benjamin Quarles credits W.E.B.DuBois as the fountainhead of leadership for Negroes at the turn of the century. In his book, *The Negro In The Making Of America,* Quarles promulgates, *"In the summer of 1905 DuBois officially launched his own movement at a meeting held at Niagara Falls, Canada. The delegates proclaimed that until they got the rights belonging to freeborn Americans, they would never cease to protest."* (Quarles 173)

The most important change was the sense that African American artists gained by being part of a group linked by ethnic pride, political activism, and a shared cultural lineage. The Harlem Renaissance symbolized the restoration of African heritage to a high place in African American consciousness. Artists during the Harlem Renaissance began to draw on African models to create a uniquely African American Art. African American artists began to enhance their racial consciousness by studying African Art and emulating its styles and themes. Artists during the Harlem Renaissance played an important role in defining the militant, self-assertive image of what came to be called the "New Negro." African Americans regarded themselves as no longer needing to be subservient but aggressively urbane. The Artists as Activists during the Harlem Renaissance is full of action. Yes, Dramatic, Action to Act!

The rhetorical critic Kenneth Burke denotes in his article, "Dramatism", published in *The International Encyclopedia of the Social Sciences,* "The dramatistic approach is implicit in the key "act." "Act" is thus a center from which many related considerations can be shown to "radiate." (Burke 445)

Unstable, harsh conditions, poverty and lynchings enabled African Americans to flee the vicious oppression in the South to settle in the Harlem neighborhoods.

The horrific brutality inflicted upon African Americans is the reason Blacks responded to the act of oppression with such urgency. Beth Eddy discusses in her book, *The Rites of Identity: The Religious Naturalism and Cultural Criticism of Kenneth Burke and Ralph Ellison,* the American identity and the social, symbolic and rhetorical rituals that produce and define it. Eddy asserts, "Rite of lynching a tragic culmination of white pride born of an American hierarchical psychosis is expressed through the ritualized attempts to exclude, eliminate, anything deemed either an infringement upon control or an affront to the status quo." (Eddy 116)

Therefore, a diverse community developed that included both African Americans who had lived in other parts of New York City for generations and a large number of Blacks from the Caribbean. An aura of confidence and creativity occurred in the northern cities as African Americans journeyed to the urban areas during the 1920s. In Harlem, the Black population produced artists, writers, musicians, orators, dramatists, and entertainers of such great talents and with so much authenticity that the period was called the Harlem Renaissance.

Lasting into the 1940s, the Harlem Renaissance was localized in New York but its impact was far-ranging. The Harlem Renaissance had a significant impact upon the writers of the Negritude Movement of the African Diaspora. Negritude writers such as, Cesaire, Damas, and Senghor were inspired by the Artists as Activists during the Harlem Renaissance. Lilyan Kesteloot in her book, *The International Influence, History of Negro African Literature*, gives evidence to this argument. (Kesteloot 3)

Displaying the cultural and creative abilities of the African American community, writers and artists from various parts of the nation descended upon Harlem. Indeed, the name of the community was synonymous with all that was best in the African American population. Small communities in many cities identified themselves as Harlem. There were Harlem cookies, Harlem books, Harlem behaviors, and Harlem attitudes. Harlem was in vogue.

The best of the poets, the jazz and blues classicists, the choreographers and dancers with something new to demonstrate, and the plastic artists and drama-tists who wanted to show the world what the African American had achieved in the art world since the emancipation, came to this community in droves. This was an upbeat time, the people were optimistic, the rhetoric was visionary, and the streets were lively.

REVIEW OF THE LITERATURE
RHETORIC OF OPPRESSION VS. RHETORIC OF PROTEST

Rhetoric of Oppression

The most maligned rhetoric of oppression was D.W. Griffith's *Birth of A Nation* (1915). W.E.B. DuBois and the N.A.A.C.P. staged vehement protests, marches and boycotts against *Birth of A Nation*. A controversial, explicitly racist American film, all describe producer/director D.W. Griffith's epic. The domestic melodrama originally premiered with the title *The Clansman* in January, 1915 in California, but three months later was retitled with the present title at its world premiere in New York. The film was based on former North

Carolina Baptist minister Rev. Thomas Dixon Jr.'s anti-black, racist philosophy about African Americans which he wrote about in his novel.

The subject matter of the film provoked immediate criticism from the National Association for the Advancement of Colored People (NAACP) for its racist portrayal of Blacks and proclamation of miscegenation, and two scenes were cut (a love scene between a Reconstructionist Senator and his mulatto mistress, and a fight scene). But the film continued to be renounced as "the meanest vilification of the Negro race." Riots broke out in major cities and it was denied release in many others. Subsequent lawsuits and picketing followed the film for years when it was re-released (in 1924, 1931, and 1938).

R. Wohlforth writes in *"In and Out of The Birth of A Nation"* examines how representatives of the NAACP demonstrated against the film, and explains D.W Griffiths attitude towards slavery and the Ku Klux Klan.

John C. Inscoe writes in *"The Clansman on Stage and Screen"*, Dixon, a native North Carolinian, promoted a theory of racial inferiority and retrogression in which blacks were devolving to a bestial state. Dixon wanted total segregation between blacks and whites. *The Clansman* tapped racial undercurrents. An all-white cast stereotypically portrayed blacks as either simple-minded or a threat to society. Dixon was pleased by the enthusiastic response and, a decade later, expected a similar reaction to the film version; he was disappointed. The black characters portrayed in the film *The Birth of A Nation* are denied normal characteristics.

Brian Gallagher in *"Racist Ideology and Black Abnormality in The Birth of a Nation"* writes, *"Blacks are defined and limited by their inevitable and inherent excesses."* The ineffectuality of blacks is a constant theme of the movie. (Gallagher 3).

Michael Rogin in "The Sword Became a Flashing Vision: D.W. Griffith's The Birth of A Nation", provides a psychohistory of Griffith and his films by examining the origins of the filmmaker's racism.

Robert Armour in "History Written in Jagged Lightning: Realistic South vs. Romantic South in The Birth of A Nation", discusses filmmaker D.W. Griffith's motives behind his film The Birth of A Nation (1915). Griffith sincerely wanted to make a film depicting the truth about the Civil War as seen by the Southerner. However, his idealized view of the South, was a racist view of the South.

100 Years of Lynching by Ralph Ginzburg, presents vivid newspaper accounts of a red record of racial atrocities. That Blacks are killed in the streets of New York while being beaten and harassed in the hills of Georgia, should come as no surprise. America has a long but seldom discussed history of violence against its Black citizens. The typical American response has been to ignore this history. A perfect example of this text can be found in the *New York Herald Tribune* dispatch of February 9, 1936, which tells of the mob hanging of a Negro, allegedly for attempted rape. These vicious lynchings made up the fabric of America, especially during the Harlem Renaissance. DuBois lead the bitter fight against lynchings in the United States during the Harlem Renaissance of the 1920s and 1930s. The articles published in the *Crisis Magazine* are a voice of protest against the vehement oppression of lynchings in the United States.

Rhetoric of Protest

W.E.B. DuBois was the most important leader of African American protest in the United States. During the early 1900s, he became the leading Black opponent of racial discrimination. In the summer of 1905 the "Niagara Movement" was formed. It objectives were to promote civil rights and put an end to race, class and culture discrimination. In 1909 all members of the Niagara Movement merged with some white citizens. The National Association for the Advancement of Colored People (NAACP) was established. The key route for dispensing NAACP policy and news pertaining to Blacks was the *Crisis* magazine. DuBois was the editor-in-chief of this publication for twenty-five years. With the *Crisis* as his rhetorical vehicle, he was able to use this magazine as his platform for protest. Benjamin Quarles argues, "Two kindred groups-the Niagara Movement and the N.A.A.C.P.-had a binding tie, W.E.B. DuBois, who was to be almost as dominant a figure in one as he had been in the other" (Quarles 174).

Clearly, DuBois and the Artists as Activists during the Harlem Renaissance prepared the way for change, Dr. Martin Luther King Jr. and the modern day Civil Rights Movement. The rhetorical strategies of DuBois and the Artists of the Harlem Renaissance moved everyone to action, from school children to laborers to professionals to presidents to just ordinary men and women, who decided to champion what's right and just on an extraordinary level.

Historians had become aware of the growing sociological literature on racial prejudice and the "Negro Problem". A study about African Americans that had sociological implications culminated in Gunmar Myrdal's, *An American Dilemma* (1944). The rhetoric about Negro characters became stereotypes that had no place in a nation that had crushed Nazi racism and committed itself to the defense of the free world. The nineteenth-century obsession with slavery had obscured the fundamental cleavages in American society. If White Americans could understand the psychic and cultural traumas occasioned by generations of bondage, they would presumably experience the necessary sympathy and guilt to undo the wrongs of the past. Crafting a rhetoric of resistance to respond to the rhetoric of oppression deals with the theme of conflict between the oppressed and oppressors, between the weak and the powerful, between the innocent and the guilty. Even the brutal slave regime, reinforced by racist ideology could not crush the human spirit. The slaves remained a troublesome form of property, capable of resistance as well as endurance.

Because White Society has increasingly oppressed African Americans, Black Protest Rhetoric has responded to oppression (demeaning rhetorical artifacts) with a sense of urgency as to deconstruct Eurocentric Political, Social, Economic, and Cultural Hegemony. This charge of rhetorical protest was lead by W.E.B. DuBois and the artists of the Harlem Renaissance. DuBois and the Harlem Renaissance artists increasingly motivated Blacks emotionally to seek social change in their daily lives. By protesting against racism, African Americans thriving against the odds (oppression) became a symbol or model for all oppressed groups. Burke indicates that, "Rhetoric deals with the possibilities of classification in its partisan aspects; it considers the ways in which individuals are at odds with one another, or become identified with groups more or less at odds with one another" (Burke, *Rhetoric of Motives*, 546).

This new contribution to knowledge fosters further implications for diversity, multiculturalism and a concept of global village, as to live in an ecumenical way without violence and war. DuBois in "The Problem of The Twentieth Century is The Problem of the Color Line" argues, "Modern Democracy cannot succeed unless the people of different races and religions are also integrated into the democratic whole." (DuBois 5)

Crafting a rhetoric of protest to respond to the rhetoric of oppression gives rise to a powerful liberation oratorical movement of resistance rhetoric during the Harlem Renaissance. The pulpit (in the Black Church) and the lectern (in the Black School) were the loci classici, however the rhetoric of liberation/protest extended to everyday speech and presentation of self/culture (Black Pride, Black Consciousness). However, there is a great gap in the literature. No scholarship looks at the fact that W.E.B. DuBois and the writers and artists during the Harlem Renaissance, made the first rhetorical statements about civil rights. Yes, DuBois and the Harlem Renaissance writers and artists made the first organized movement with calculated rhetorical articulations. Robert Hayden writes in the preface of the text, *The New Negro* by Alain Locke, "The New Negro" articulates the crucial ideas of a generation in rebellion against accepted beliefs and engaged in racial self-discovery and cultural re-assessment." (Locke xiii)

As evidence to this fact, also note, pictures of DuBois, Garvey, The Black Cross Nurses and other Harlem Negroes protesting and marching through the streets of Harlem in the 1920s and 1930s. Also, the Artists as Activists during the Harlem Renaissance created a movement of social protest by establishing the NAACP long before Dr. King. However, King gets all the credit for the rhetorical inducements of the civil rights movement but DuBois should get the credit, as harbinger DuBois laid the foundation for Dr. King and the modern civil rights movement. According to Roi Ottley, in his book, *Black Odyssey*, " DuBois became a towering figure in Negro life, DuBois' belief in his cause and indefatigable work in advancing it explains much of the N.A.A.C.P.'s. success" (Ottley 221).

I have looked at research in the field of African American History and Culture, Critical and Cultural Studies and Rhetoric and Communications Studies and no scholarship credits DuBois with laying the foundations of the modern day civil rights movement or by organizing the Niagara Movement, which is today called the N.A.A.C.P. Credit is only given to Dr. Martin Luther King Jr., as the organizer and creator of the modern civil rights movement.

The following disquisitions do not give DuBois nor any of the Harlem Renaissance Artists credit for creating social protest. However, this study closes the gap in the literature and opens the door for further implications and theory building.

The scholarship on DuBois is vast, however, no scholarship looks at DuBois as the leader of the civil rights movement during the Harlem Renaissance and how he inspired a plethora of artists as activists during this period. In the 1960s, Francis Broderick, (1969), authored what remains as one of the most readable biographies of DuBois. In the 1970s, Meyer Weinberg, (1970), edited an insightful reader of DuBois' writings, providing us an invaluable collage of the thoughts of and the man himself.Of course, some criticism of DuBois can be found in works exclusive to African American subjects. However, such works make mention of DuBois or reference his work insofar as they relate to the primary topic. For example, August Meiers's text, *Negro Thought in America* explores the racial thought of the times in which Booker T. Washington emerged as a significant "Negro" leader. Chapter 11 of that text considers "The Paradox of W.E.B. DuBois inasmuch as DuBois represented a philosophical position antithetical to Washington's.

There are various dissertation abstracts, journal articles and essays available to this study, yet, following the same pattern of broad and indirect references to DuBois. Most do not feature DuBois as a Harlem Renaissance, Civil Rights Leader nor do they feature his famous book, *The Souls of Black Folk*, nor his great rhetorical articles and speeches published in the *Crisis Magazine*. However, I shall uncover these rhetorical gems of DuBoisian thought.

The African American rhetor, like any other rhetor, digs into his cultural/ethnic roots for his/her communicative devices. Bernard Bell's *The Folk Roots of Contemporary Afro-American Literature*, for example, takes a close look at the folk traditions of African American people, i.e. their religion and music, and how these traditions greatly influence African American communication. Bell gives an abundance of examples to illustrate that "African American contemporary communication is rooted deeply in the folk art tradition."[14]

To show an increasing international urgency for a Black Protest Rhetoric the French writer Jean-Paul Sartre contends, "Black Culture is functional, if it answers a need which is defined in precise terms and if all writers attempt to treat the Black soul."[15]   Sartre is saying that writers of other cultures should write about the Black experience, as Black culture is full of depth and soul.

Furthermore, the rhetor speaking about the African American experience, in order to get the essence of that experience, must rely on the folk tradition of the people he/she writes about.

Sterling Brown, author, essayist—argues that it is necessary for the African American writer to go back to his roots if he is to give an accurate portrayal of Black folks. Brown himself wrote about Southern rural Black folks; so he traveled extensively in the South to get firsthand accounts about his people. Other writers were also beginning to write from their cultural roots, and this trend among African American writers was leading them away from the classical tradition of rhetoric. It was of course during the Harlem Renaissance that the African American critic Sterling Brown emphasized that the African American writers are more assured, more self-reliant, and are less taken in by American hypocrisy and express their protest now with irony, with anger, seldom with humility. They do not flinch from an honest portrayal of folk life. Therefore, this new philosophical stance, or perhaps political stance, affected a new rhetoric which, according to Brown, had five concerns: "1. A discovery of Africa as a source of race pride, 2. A use of Black heroes and heroic episodes from American History,"[16] "3. Propaganda or protest, 4. A treatment of Black masses with more understanding and less apology and 5. Franker and deeper self-revelation."[17]

In addition to believing that the African American rhetor should draw upon his cultural tradition, there are those critics who believe that African American communication differs in its aims and methods, and since the African American rhetor speaks for an African American audience, this communication for the people should come from the African American experience. This philosophy is expressed in the writings of reputable critics such as James Emanuel, Abraham Chapman and Nick Aaron Ford—to name a few—whose essays are anthologized in Lloyd W. Brown's *The Black Writer in Africa and the Americas*. Nick A. Ford's essay quotes Larry Neal as saying, "it (the Black Arts Movement) envisions an art that speaks directly to the needs and aspirations of Black America. It proposes a separate symbolism, mythology, and iconology."[18] One who examines the rhetors of the modern period will conclude that a similar kind of militancy was beginning to emerge. According to Stephen Bronz, many Black rhetors, in order to bolster their racial pride, sought out their cultural roots either in the African American past or among lower class African Americans. Then there were those who looked to the cultures of pre-colonial and colonial Africa for their heritage. Bronz argues that with this interest in racial heritage, Black rhetors now "had subjects and feelings to write about, but their problem was to find a useful traditional form and language."[19]

Evidently, finding a tradition, form, and language was no problem for James Weldon Johnson because his interest in his heritage motivated him to write *God's Trombones*. Johnson wrote this book of speeches and sermons as a guide to help younger African American rhetors in expressing their own heritage. The volume abounds with folk imagery. Johnson himself writes in the Preface to *The Book of American Negro Poetry*, "folk tradition provides unfailing sources of material for authentic speech. I myself did a similar thing in writing *God's Trombones*. I went back to the genuine folk stuff that clings around the old-time Negro preacher..."[20] Also, Johnson advocates using the dialect which he describes as the "common, racy, living authentic speech of the Negro in certain phases of real life."[21]

Paul L. Dunbar, Sterling Brown, Langston Hughes, and many of their successors used the authentic speech of the common folks. Dunbar's dialect was his portrayal of the common Negro speech style.

Jean Wagner's comprehensive study of the Harlem Renaissance lists those who got their imagistic language and verse forms from the Negro folk tradition, such as the sermons, worksongs, blues, jazz and other music forms. To illustrate his point, Wagner quotes Langston Hughes who was known as the writer of jazz: "Jazz to me is one of the inherent expressions of Negro life in America; the eternal tom-tom beating in the Negro soul—the tom-tom of revolt..."[22] One of the recurring themes in Eugene Redmond's *Drumvoices* is that most rhetorical principles often depend on music for their language and structure. Many critics, in addition to Wagner and Redmond, attest to the fact that African American writing and speaking are very close kin to music.

Included in this research study are at least four authors who support this "kinship" theory between Black Language and Black Music: Blyden Jackson, Louis Rubin, Margaret Perry, Stephen Henderson, and Geneva Smitherman. Not only do these authors support this "kinship" theory in their books, but they also illustrate with detailed examples how African American rhetors have drawn from this relationship of music and communication to authenticate their rhetoric as it represents African American life. Stephen Henderson agrees, "that Black music lies at the basis of much of Black rhetoric, either consciously or covertly."[23]

Jean Wagner concludes that jazz as the favorite expression of Black folk also became the favorite means of expressing the rebellious spirit of the Negro. Therefore, to any scholar of African American Communication, it is understandable that this rebellious spirit should be imitated in the rhetorical articulations.

As evidenced by the examples given, many of the African American rhetors of the Harlem Renaissance had begun to abandon the classical traditional forms and language of western civilization and had begun to go to the folk tradition of their own culture or, in some instances, to Africa for language and form. It was as if the African American rhetors were answering the plea of James Weldon Johnson when he wrote in 1925 that, "...the colored writer in the United States needs to find a form that will express the racial spirit by symbols."[24] By the end of the Harlem Renaissance, Johnson's challenge was being met.

Rhys H. Williams, in his article, "Social Movement Theory, Cultural Resources in Strategy and Organization," argues, "for the usefulness of approaching social movement ideology as a set of cultural resources."[25]

METHODOLOGY

The methodology utilized in this dissertation will examine and discover who are the Artists as Activists during the 1920s and 1930s. And how is their Art a statement of Social Protest, which gave rise to the movement known as the Harlem Renaissance. The methodology is grounded theory in rhetorical criticism, engaging the philosophical discourse of Kenneth Burke. The works of W.E.B. DuBois and the Artists of the Harlem Renaissance are examined, concentrating upon the development of their respective artistic accomplishments. This dissertation is an original critical analysis of a significant rhetorical artifact; the artists and their art from The New Negro Movement known as the Black Renaissance or Harlem Renaissance. The philosophical discourse of Kenneth

Burke is the legitimate critical methodology, which serves to open up the artifact for the audience. Each chapter will include: 1. A Biographical sketch of each Artist 2. The Environment, what is going on in society/the social fabric. 3. The philosophical thought and protest work of the Artist. 4. A Burkean Analysis and 5. Conclusions and Implications for future study.

Contemporary rhetorical criticism should attempt to integrate language symbols that persuade through symbolic action and identification. The process moves from inside the text to reader response to the writer's world. What the contemporary rhetorical critic does with these forms of criticism is to make interrelationships clear by revealing the identification that interlocks the triangle of work-reader-writer. Rhetorical criticism concerns itself not only with what the work is but what it might be. The rhetorical critic's quest, then, is to discover not how good the work is but what its significance is and how it achieves that significance.

Kenneth Burke comes closest to forming a complete critical theory, as his philosophical discourse is engaged in examining identification, dramatism and the pentad. One such area of investigation is the persuasive power of slavery, racism and oppression. How these Harlem Renaissance artists purged their emotions of oppression and created artistic protest rhetoric. Using the work of Kenneth Burke as a basis, the study entails the search for slavery, racism and oppression-and the overarching rhetorical vision using the methodological construct proposed by Burke. In order to place the art as protest rhetoric of DuBois and the artist of the Harlem Renaissance into a compact and concise theoretical framework I selected the rhetorical criticism by Kenneth Burke.As Kenneth Burke was born in 1897 he lived during the Harlem Renaissance and was a good friend of Ralph Ellison, Harlem Renaissance author of *Invisible Man*. Burke's rhetoric takes on an increasingly interesting literary, artistic and dramatic flourish that is truly apropos to the study of protest rhetoric during the Harlem Renaissance. Beth Eddy in her text, *The Rites of Identity: The Religious Naturalism and Cultural Criticism of Kenneth Burke and Ralph Ellison,* argues, "this tradition provides useful means for understanding what is currently true about human identities and differences" (186). As Ellison is a writer during the Harlem Renaissance, Burke's philosophical discourse, therefore, becomes the critical apparatus, conceptual framework or organizing glue of this dissertation.

The African American protest rhetoric selected for this study is that rhetoric of African Americans who object to the social, economic, political and cultural discrimination suffered by African Americans in the United States during the Harlem Renaissance. W.E.B. DuBois and the artists of the Harlem Renaissance will be examined, as they have been ignored, marginalized and obscured by the academy. Finally, as with any research, perhaps there are questions/problems that have not been resolved fully and, therefore, will provide thought for further research.

As the Harlem Renaissance is a great period of artistic African American life and culture, I have fashioned a pedagogical research tool in the performing arts. The categories I will examine are: Literature, Dance, Music, Theatre and

Film, from each area I have selected famous and not so famous African Americans. I have selected many obscure and unknown African Americans, because our educational system has a Eurocentric thrust. The contributions of these Blacks are not taught in schools, except during Black History Month in February, when we hear of a few! Therefore, this study is a critical assessment of African American culture and aesthetics based upon an Afro-centric approach to Black Identity, Black Consciousness, Black Pride, Black Culture.

Artists during the Harlem Renaissance were also Civil Rights Activists. They deconstructed a plethora of barriers and paved the way for generations of African Americans to rise towards the struggle and prove that African Americans are just as good, just as educated, just as hardworking and just as decent as the white man; African Americans have made significant accomplishments in all fields of endeavor. These artistic harbingers overcame adversity and became successful against the odds of racism, segregation, prejudice, hatred, oppression and bigotry in the so-called land of the free, and home of the brave, USA. Many of these artists became expatriates and considered Europe their home, as they could perform there in a free and open racial environment.

This study seeks to demonstrate that Black Protest Rhetoric during the Harlem Renaissance is an inducement strategy to persuade African Americans to create their own artistic forms of political, social and economic liberation.

DuBois and the Artists during the Harlem Renaissance laid the foundation for Martin Luther King Jr. and the modern day civil rights movement. This study seeks to discover how W.E.B. DuBois and the Artists of the Harlem Renaissance articulated their message? What were their rhetorical strategies, persuasive appeals and how did their rhetoric and art create symbolic action, thus, motivating African Americans to protest for change of the status quo. How did W.E.B. DuBois and the Artists of the Harlem Renaissance protest against hegemony? (Race, Class, Culture, Gender).

I seek to make a contribution to knowledge with a ground-breaking study that is expository, novel and analytical examining obscured, marginalized, silent voices that have been neglected and fallen into the crevices of history. I will examine the signals, signs, and significations of these Artists as Activists works as social protest.

NOTES

1. Hoyt Fuller "Blacks Need Black Culture," *Spectator Newspaper*. University of Iowa, 1975. p.1.

2. Hoyt Fuller, p.1

3. Grace Holt, "Metaphor, Black Discourse Style, and Cultural Reality," in *Ebonics: The Language of Black Folks*. (Ed.) Robert L. Williams. St. Louis: Institute of Black Studies, 1975, p.88.

4. Richard Barksdale and Kenneth Kinnamon, *Black Writers of America: A Comprehensive Anthology.* New York: Macmillan, 1972, p.479.

5. Ralph W. Ellison, *Invisible Man.* New York: Random House, 1947, p.231.

6. Larry Neal, "The Black Arts Movement," in *Calvacade: Negro American Writing From 1760 to the Present.* (Ed.) Arthur P. Davis and Saunders Redding. New York: Houghton Mifflin, 1971, p.798.

7. Don L. Lee, *Dynamite Voices I: Black Poets of the Sixties.* Detroit: Broadside Press 1971 p.25.

8. Stephen Henderson, *The Militant Black Writer in Africa and the United States.* Madison, Wisconsin: University of Wisconsin Press, 1969, p.65.

9. Grace S. Holt, "Inversion In Black Communication" in *Communication in Urban Black America.*(Ed.) Thomas Kochman. Urbana, Illinois: University of Illinois Press, 1972 p.158.

10. Johnson, p.6

11. Craig Werner, "Blues for T.S. Eliot and Langston Hughes: The Afro-Modernist Aesthetic of Harlem Gallery," *Black American Literature Forum* vol.24, 1990, p. 45.

12. Werner, p. 46.

13. Brown, p. 78

14. Bernard Bell, *The Folk Roots of Contemporary Afro-American Literature.* Detroit: Broadside Press, 1974, p.2.

15. Jean-Paul Sartre, "Black Orpheus," in *Black American Writer.* (Ed.) C. Bigsby. Baltimore: Penguin Books, 1971, p.11.

16. Sterling Brown, *Negro Literature and Drama.* New York: Atheneum, 1972, p.79.

17. Sterling Brown, p.61.

18. Nick A. Ford, "The Problem of Evaluation," in *The Black Writer in Africa and the Americas.* (Ed.) Lloyd Brown, Los Angeles: Hennessey and Ingalls, 1973, p.55

19. Stephen Bronz, *Roots of Black Racial Consciousness.* New York: Libra, 1964, p.5.

20. James Weldon Johnson, *The Book of American Negro Poetry.* New York: Harcourt, Brace and Company, 1922, p.6.

21. Johnson, p.4.

22. Jean Wagner, *Les Poetes Negres Des Etats-Unis.* Paris: Sorbonne University Press, 1963, p.2.

23. Henderson, p.66.

24. Johnson, p.4

25. Rhys H. William, "Social Movement Theory and Cultural Resources," *Strategy and Organization* vol.180, 1992, p.1.

2

THE WORLD OF LITERATURE

JESSIE REDMON FAUSET

American novelist, editor, short story writer, critic, essayist, poet, and writer of children's stories. She was an integral figure of the Harlem Renaissance-a period of great achievement in African American art and literature that developed an African American identity. Fauset earned recognition for her work on the Crisis, a progressive magazine published by the National Association for the Advancement of Colored People. As literary editor of the Crisis, Fauset discovered and published early works by such authors as Langston Hughes, Jean Toomer, and Claude McKay. She also wrote short stories and novels that were originally categorized as romantic melodramas but are now regarded as pioneering advocations of feminism and civil rights. According to Benjamin Quarles, in his book, *The Negro In The Making Of America*, "Miss. Fauset dealt with problems of the color line but her characters were respectable members of the educated middle class."(Quarles 201). It was very bold and daring for Fauset to write about the Negro Middle Class, as during this time Blacks were thought of as inferior. Tracing the lives of upper middle-class black families, Fauset often centered upon a light-skinned heroine's efforts to gain economic security and social status by passing for white. Many of Fauset's protagonists subsequently suffer anguish as a result of bringing false values upon themselves and their families. Fauset challenged conventional literary portraits of females by featuring women who actively pursued careers and sought equality in their relationships with men. Her discussions of racial and sexual discrimination are considered insightful social commentaries, for the time.

Fauset was born to Reverend Redmon, an outspoken African-Methodist minister, and Annie (Seamon) Fauset in Philadelphia in 1882. Fauset attended Philadelphia public schools and was graduated from the High School for Girls in 1900. She enrolled at Cornell University and became the first black woman at the University to win Phi Beta Kappa honors upon her graduation. For the next fourteen years she taught at various schools, including Douglass High School in Baltimore and Dunbar High School in Washington, D.C. In 1919 she received a Master of Arts degree from the University of Pennsylvania, the same year she joined the staff of the *Crisis*. Along with W.E.B. DuBois, she also produced the *Brownies' Book*, a monthly magazine for black children, to which she contributed many of her own stories. In 1921 DuBois sent Fauset to Europe to cover the second Pan-African Congress in London, Brussels, and Paris; she was so enamored of Paris that she remained there for a year, studying French at the Sorbonne. Upon her return to the United States, she quit her position at the *Crisis* and, unable to find employment as a "publisher's reader" or a "social secretary" as she had hoped, returned to teaching in 1926. (Feeney 20). She married Herbert E. Harris, an insurance agent and businessman, several years later. Toward the end of her life she traveled extensively and taught English at Hampton Institute and Latin and French at Tuskegee Institute. She died in Philadelphia in 1961.

Fauset's Career as a novelist began after reading T.S. Stribling's *Birthright*, a highly regarded novel about a mulatto Harvard graduate's inability to bring cultural refinement to the residents of his Tennessee hometown. When *Birthright* was first published in 1922, critics praised it as the most significant novel on the Negro written by a white American. Dismayed by the "fallacies" she found in Stribling's book, Fauset resolved to write a book about Negro life: "A number of us started writing at that time... Nella Larsen and Walter White, for instance, were affected just as I was. We reasoned, ' Here is an audience waiting to hear the truth about us. Let us who are better qualified to present the truth than any white writer, try to do so" (Lewis 375). In 1924 Fauset published her first novel, *There is Confusion*. The work depicts two wealthy black Philadelphia families who are brought together by the marriage of their children. Instead of focusing on the differences between black and white society, however, Fauset portrayed their similarities. While some critics faulted the book for an enigmatic narrative and melodramatic dialogue, the numerous characters, storylines, and details in *There Is Confusion* prompted William Stanley Braithwaite to describe Fauset as "the potential Jane Austen of Negro literature."(Braithwaite 22)   Sylvander observed: "By taking the traditional Bildungsroman and family novel pattern and adapting them to study the peculiar confusion, learning, and ultimate understanding of American Blacks, Fauset has revealed insight into the human experience."(Sylvander 24)

There is Confusion, explores the limited vocational alternatives available to women, especially black women, and also shows women breaking out of these limits without being excessively punished. The novel explores the racial discrimination and socio-cultural inheritance faced by the northern urban black, and it depicts a wide range of characters and actions against a backdrop of American slave history and racially mixed heredity. Fauset subtly explores alternatives to society's sometimes limiting norms. She looks upon religion in the black church, for example, as a social institution capable of giving support to people with a variety of problems, rather than as a received body of supernatural truth. Similarly, biblical motifs are used for their historical significance, not their religious significance. Black folk material as the basis for individuality in black art is demonstrated in Joanna's use of a black children's dance-games as her entree into the theatrical world. If one theme could be said to dominate *There is Confusion*, it is that surviving the hardships engendered by discrimination places the black person and the race in a position of superiority. As the character Brian says:

> The complex of color...every colored man feels it sooner or later. It gets in the way of his dreams, of his education, of his marriage, of the rearing of his children. The time comes when he thinks, 'I might just as well fall back; there's no use pushing one. A colored man just can't make any headway in this awful country.' Of course, it's a fallacy. And if a fellow sticks it out he finally gets past it, but not before it has worked considerable confusion in his life. To have the ordinary job of living is bad enough, but to add to it all the thousand and one difficulties which follow simply in the train of being colored-well, all I've got to say, Sylvia, is we're some wonderful people to live through it all and keep our sanity.(Fauset, There is Confusion, 29).

There is Confusion received generally favorable reviews. A *New York Times Book Review* pointed to the novelty of its having been written by a college-educated Negro woman, and the December 1924 *London Times Literary Supplement* found the novel an "able and unusual story" which charmed the English reader by its "apt allusions to circumstances of Negro life." (Review, LTLS, 1924, 78).

Critical readings of *There is Confusion* since its first publication have concentrated narrowly, and often erroneously, on Fauset's depiction of black middle-class characters. Arthur P. Davis, for example, in his 1974 book, *From the Dark Tower: Afro-American Writers 1900-1960* (1974), calls Fauset the "most prolific, and in many ways the most representative, of the glorifiers of the Negro middle class," and calls *There is Confusion* her "fullest and most representative novel", because it renders "more of the typical attitudes and shibboleths held by the New Negro middle class of the 1920's than any of her others." Davis concludes, "She is really trying to make a very small group of Negroes represent all Negroes." (Davis 25). While Fauset sympathizes with the black bourgeoisie, Lee R. Edwards and Arlyn Diamond points out that Fauset also "realizes the potential sterility and destructiveness of their overwhelming concern with whiteness and respectability." (Edwards 30).

Many formal devices in *Plum Bun* make it, in many ways, her best work. She corrects the glaring structural weaknesses of her first novel by concentrating in the second one on a major character, Angela Murray, from whose point of view the story is told. Time spans and time transitions in *Plum Bun* are shorter and smoother than they were in *There is Confusion*. The external world is described in more detail and is used to complement Angela's changing perceptions as she goes from an ambitious and attractive young mulatto who passes for white to a mature and sensitive artist claiming her black heritage.

The Murray family is not as wealthy as the Marshalls of *There is Confusion*, and the theme of importance of family, of roots, of enduring and honest relationships is made separate from the social and economic class of the characters. Fauset continues to treat racial discrimination in her second novel but concentrates on the peculiar ironies of discrimination against the "black" who is, by all appearances, white. The focus, again, is not simply on the discrimination, but on the various ways characters develop from having to deal with historical, biological, psychological and economic realities. Angela Murray's psychology-her decision to pass and her subsequent decision to reclaim her racial heritage-is fully explored. In focusing on Angela, Fauset is able to explore fully the limitations of gender roles, as well as women's attempts to break free of some of those roles.

Fauset's title is taken from the second stanza of a nursery rhyme, which also provides the book's epigraph: "To market, to market/To buy a Plum Bun;/ Home again, Home again,/Market is done." The first section of the novel, "Home," describes the Murray family life on Opal Street in Philadelphia, the death of Angela's parents, the differences between the dark sister, Virginia, and Angela, who decides to go to New York and pass for white. The seven chapters of the second section, "Market" open with Angela's arrival in New York and end with Virginia's arrival there. The third section, "Plum Bun," is devoted to Angela's affair with the rich, white Roger Fielding. "Home Again," the fourth and long section, is spent exploring Angela's attempts to establish meaningful and lasting relationships with carefully chosen men and women in her life. In the short final section, "Market is Done," Angela, a painter, is awarded a trip to France, but reveals her racial identity in response to reporters' badgering of a black woman, Miss Powell. For her honesty, Angela is ultimately rewarded with a Paris reunion with her true love, Anthony Cross, who has lingered in the background in triple disguise as a poor black who looks white.

Plum Bun is a frequently misunderstood, but carefully constructed African-American Bildungsroman in which racial difference is the societal barrier perceived by the growing central character first as an absolute and, finally, as a false distinction of value to be overcome, ignored, and replaced. In American society, where class does not loom as the unalterable state reasonably imposed upon a character, unchangeable skin color becomes the social tool for discrimination. *Plum Bun* is an American romance which satirizes traditional romantic assumptions, particularly in regard to race and sex. Black Blood is customarily a bar sinister to American romance. Angela sees it in just that way at the beginning of the novel; her romantic ideals of adventure and love point directly toward being white, and marrying white as well as rich. While she believes in the American fairy-tale romance, marriage with her white prince, Roger Fielding, eludes her. It is only when Angela has come to a new understanding of skin color, money and marriage that Roger arrives at her door with his marriage offer; he is, of course, no longer a prince to Angela, for he represents none of her new and true ideals.

Jessie Fauset's last two novels contain some departures from the content and form of her first two. *The Chinaberry Tree* (1931) and *Comedy, American Style* (1933) are more significant in showing Fauset's intentions.

In *The Chinaberry Tree: A Novel of American Life* (1931), Fauset again explored the psychological consequences of racism on blacks. This book revolves around three characters of mixed racial ancestry who are denied social respectability by narrow-minded residents of a small town. Fauset's blend of tragedy and romance garnered complimentary reviews upon the novel's publication.

The plot of *The Chinaberry Tree* is based on a story Fauset had heard when she was fifteen, and which she had written as a short story. "Double Trouble." She wrote the novel in the summer of 1931, while she was taking a French class at Columbia University. During the academic year, Fauset was teaching at De Witt Clinton High School.

In *The Chinaberry Tree*, Fauset explores "the homelife of the colored American who is not being pressed too hard by the Furies of Prejudice, Ignorance, and Economic Injustice." The Frederick A. Stokes Company, which had published *Plum Bun*, balked a bit at *The Chinaberry Tree*, agreeing to publish it only after Fauset succeeded in getting Zona Gale to write an introduction. Readers at Stokes, Fauset wrote to Gale on 20 October 1931, "declare plainly that there ain't no such colored people as these, who speak decent English, are self-supporting and have a few ideals." (Sylvander 27).

A small New Jersey community named Red Brook provides the setting for the exploration of values in *The Chinaberry Tree*. White townspeople appear in only one scene in the book, as onlookers at a community skating party. It is black Red Brook society which has over the years ostracized mulatto Aunt Sal Strange, lover of the deceased Colonel Halloway, for bearing Laurentine out of wedlock. The beautiful Laurentine has grown up oversensitive to what an unwitting small playmate once called her "bad blood," and she seeks to overcome the past by marriage to a respectable man.

Despite the demands of her teaching career on her time, Fauset wrote one more novel, published in 1933, when she was fifty-one years old. *Comedy, American Style* focuses on the ironies of American black life with more directness and less sentimentality than any of her previous novels, and it includes more characters who do not succeed in attaining true understanding. Fauset's depiction of Olivia Cary, the mother in this novel, has been called "the most penetrating study of color mania in American fiction" (Gloster 37).

All of Olivia Cary's actions stem from her hatred of being black and her desire to be white. Fauset is not totally convincing in explaining the motivation for this color mania, although she does provide some insight into this character when she reveals that Janet Blanchard, Olivia's mother, is strongly class conscious, and that the young Olivia takes pleasure at being mistaken for a little Italian girl. She marries a doctor, Christopher Cary, who, while light enough to pass for white, never exercises that option.

Three of the Cary family are destroyed by Olivia's color mania. Oliver becomes a young suicide. Teresa, forced to marry a man she does not love dies emotionally. Olivia lives on in eventual isolation and poverty. Only the father and young Christopher overcome and survive, through much pain and difficulty, the damage Olivia causes. Showing alternatives to Olivia Cary's response to American racism, Fauset locates her primary positive character outside the family. Phebe Grant is a blond and blue-eyed black woman of the lowest social class who plays no games with her racial inheritance. "I belong to the black or Negro race," she responds to a teacher at a young age. When she is older, and having risen from a seamstress with a white family to a shop-owning modiste, Phebe refuses to marry a rich white man on false pretenses. Finally, after a mature and responsible marriage to the young Christopher Cary, she remains absolutely loyal through intense temptation.

For these struggling characters-the elder and younger Christophers and Phebe-there is a kind of happy ending, at least a temporary victory over their trials and an increased strength from having endured. There is no easy way of dealing successfully with life or race in America, Fauset reminds her readers, but there are alternatives to Olivia Cary's imitation of white life. Phebe Grant's alternative is acceptance of her inheritance, hard work, unswerving loyalty and honesty.

Jessie Fauset's influence on black art in the period of the Harlem Renaissance was extensive. Nevertheless, her work has been dismissed frequently by white critics who have erroneously assumed her novels reflect her easy early life and who believe she is simply promoting the black middle class. More accurately Fauset's work reflects the growth of a struggling, self-made, sophisticated, widely read and deliberate literary artist, whose thematic concerns and formal experiments are worth critical investigation. Fauset's essays reveal her curiosity and sympathy, but the novels, too, leave an impression of strength gained through difficulties overcome. Far from promoting a limited notion of respectability, Fauset emphasizes recognition of a morality which is at variance with society's codes. Fauset's strength may lie in her unobtrusive presentation of alternatives for defining the black American woman: more exploratory than dogmatic, more searching than protesting.

In describing Jessie Redmon Fauset and her role in helping the field of black literature, Langston Hughes remarked: "Jessie Fauset at the *Crisis*, Charles S. Johnson at *Opportunity*, and Alain Locke in Washington were the three people who mid-wifed the so-called New Negro Literature into being. Kind and critical-but not too critical for the young-they nursed us along until our books were born." (Hughes 27).

JAMES WELDON JOHNSON

Versatility is the most salient characteristic of the life and career of James Weldon Johnson. Equipped with restless intelligence, abundant energy, and an abhorrence of spare time, he crowded almost a dozen occupations into a busy lifetime, excelling in most of them: teacher, school principal, journalist, lawyer, songwriter, diplomat, novelist, poet, civil rights crusader, anthologist, professor. Throughout his various activities three concerns persisted. First, he was usually involved in education in one way or another, viewing it both as a route to individual achievement and as a means of racial advancement. Second, he devoted his considerable talents mainly to the service of his race, notably during his decade and a half as a major leader of the National Association for the Advancement of Colored People (1916-1930), and in other ways at other times of his life. Third, through his belletristic writing and his anthologies he was both contributor to and preserver of the Afro-American literary tradition, linking the nineteenth century to the Harlem Renaissance.

Johnson's family background encouraged achievement and cultural pursuits. His father, James Johnson, was a self-educated man who, as a waiter in New York and a head waiter in Nassau and then in Jacksonville, Florida, achieved economic security and adopted middle-class values. While in New York he met and courted Helen Louise Dillet, a young woman of African-French-English ancestry, a native of Nassau who had grown up in New York, received a good education, and developed her musical talent. When Dillet returned with her mother to her native island in 1861, James Johnson followed her and secured a position in a large hotel. They were married in 1864 and prospered initially, but an economic recession forced the couple and their infant daughter to move to Jacksonville, a rapidly expanding city becoming an important tourist center. Here were born James William (changed in 1913 to Weldon) Johnson and, two years later, John Rosamond Johnson.

Growing up in an increasingly secure middle class home with books and a piano, young James was inculcated with strict notions of integrity by his father and with intellectual and artistic interests by his mother. The first black woman public school teacher in Florida, Helen Johnson encouraged a love of learning in her sons, whom she taught at home before they attained school age and again in the classroom at Stanton School. From her they learned to read and play the piano. A precocious child, James was quickly reading Charles Dickens, Sir Walter Scott, John Bunyan, and Jacob and Wilhelm Grimm. Formal education at Stanton School extended only through the eighth grade, from which James graduated in 1887, but travel and friends had a broadening effect. While still a small child he accompanied his family on a visit to Nassau, and in 1884 he spent a summer in New York with his grandmother and her sister. He took a whitmanesque pleasure in the bustling movement and noise of the great city: "I loved the ferryboats- the rushing crowds, the stamping teams and yelling teamsters, the tooting whistles, the rattling windlasses and clanging when we

left and entered the ship." (Johnson 5) As he further recalled in his autobiography, *Along This Way* (1933), "I was born to be a New Yorker." (Johnson 5). This cosmopolitan sense of self was reinforced by his friendships with Ricardo Rodriguez Ponce, a Cuban youth from whom he learned Spanish; Judson Douglass Wetmore (the "D-" of *Along This Way*), the near-white prototype for the protagonist of *The Autobiography of an Ex-Colored Man* (1912); and, somewhat later, a cultured and widely traveled white physician named Dr. Thomas Osmond Summers, for whom he worked as an assistant and with whom he traveled to Washington on a professional trip. Reading literary erotica and religious agnosticism in Dr. Summers's library, young Johnson expanded his interests in additional directions.

His development continued at Atlanta University, where he matriculated in the preparatory division after graduation from Stanton. In 1894 he received the A.B. degree from the collegiate division. At least as important as the rather rigorous academic curriculum, he received an education in racial issues from which he had been somewhat sheltered in Jacksonville. This other education included, he remembered forty years later, "preparation to meet the tasks and exigencies of life as a Negro, a realization of the peculiar responsibilities due to my own racial group, and a comprehension of the application of American democracy to Negro citizens." (Johnson 58) Not only was race a constant topic of discussion and debate among the undergraduates, but Johnson spent two summers teaching in a black rural school near Hampton, Georgia, an invaluable experience with a mode of black life new to him. In the summer before his senior year he traveled to Chicago to work in the great Columbian Exposition. Here on "Colored People's Day" he heard the aged Frederick Douglass speak and the young Paul Laurence Dunbar read from his poetry. With Dunbar, who was not yet famous, he quickly initiated a friendship and literary relation that would continue for many years thereafter.

Upon graduation and not yet twenty-three years of age, Johnson left Atlanta University as a member of a singing quartet touring New England to raise money for the institution. Back in Jacksonville in the fall as principal of Stanton, now perhaps the largest public school in the state, he was thoroughly prepared by education, travel, and experience to assume his self-defined role as "leader and helper to my race." In addition to improving Stanton by adding ninth and tenth-grade courses, he attempted to educate the city's adult black community by starting a newspaper, *The Daily American*, which was published for eight months in 1895 and 1896. In his editorials Johnson promoted racial self-help while defending civil rights for the race against the resurgence of white supremacy. The financial failure of the newspaper was disappointing, but he hoped other avenues to racial leadership could be opened. Although not a single black person had ever been admitted to the Florida bar, Johnson began to read law in the office of a friendly white attorney. After a year and a half he passed a rigorous bar examination despite the obvious racial hostility of the examiners. As a Lawyer, however, he found routine paper work tedious, and his continuing duties at Stanton occupied much of his time. Johnson was growing restless in Jacksonville, too small an arena to contain either his talents or his ambitions. Furthermore, racial restrictions were tightening as the new century began.

The pattern of Johnson's career alternated between administrative and artistic roles. He had written poetry in college and even before, and the postgraduation concert tour had revived his earlier interest in music. When his brother John returned to Jacksonville in 1897, after successfully having studied at the New England Conservatory of Music and after having completed a tour with a black variety show, James was about ready to resume creative activity. Together the brothers wrote Tolosa, or The Royal Document, which was a comic opera satirizing the new American imperialism in a Gilbert-and-Sullivan mode. James supplied the story and lyrics while his brother composed the music. A trip to New York in the summer of 1899 did not lead to the production of the work, as the brothers had hoped, but it did introduce them to some of the key figures of the musical stage, including Oscar Hammerstein. Among the celebrated black theatrical personalities they met were the comedians Bert Williams, George Walker, and Ernest Hogan and the musicians Bob Cole, Will Marion Cook, and Harry T. Burleigh. Cook had collaborated on the operetta *Clorindy, or the Origin of the Cakewalk* (1898) with Paul Laurence Dunbar, who, now famous, renewed his friendship with Johnson. The life of black bohemia in New York fascinated the schoolmaster; Jacksonville certainly had nothing comparable. "I now began to grope toward a realization of the importance of the American Negro's cultural background and his creative folk art," he was to write in *Along This Way*, "and to speculate on the superstructure of conscious art that might be reared on them." (Johnson 10)

The creative side of Johnson's personality was now in the ascendancy. While still in New York, he wrote with his brother and Bob Cole the song "Louisiana Liza," selling it to a popular white singer. Returning to Jacksonville, he wrote one of his best dialect poems, the plaintive love lyric "Sence You Went Away," which was published in *Century* in 1900, the first time the author appeared in print in a national magazine. **With his brother he shortly afterward wrote "Lift Every Voice and Sing," which was to become known as the "Negro national Anthem."** Back in New York the following summer (and the summer thereafter), the brothers formed a songwriting partnership with Bob Cole. Almost immediately successful in bringing out hit songs, the team nevertheless worked at a disadvantage with the Johnsons' in Florida most of the year. After a fire destroyed a large area of Jacksonville, including the Stanton School, and after an ugly and dangerous personal encounter with state militiamen(brought in to keep order) Johnson's hometown seemed even less attractive than before. The school was rebuilt, shoddily, and he returned to work as principal. A romance with a teacher from Tampa briefly competed with the allure of Tin Pan Alley, but in the fall of 1902 he resigned from Stanton, moved to New York, and devoted himself to the team of Cole and Johnson Brothers.

The trio produced dozens of songs, including such hits as "Under the Bamboo Tree," "The Congo Love Song," "My Castle on the Nile," "I Ain't Gwinter Work No Mo'," "The Maiden with the Dreamy Eyes," "Nobody's Lookin' But de Owl and de Moon," "I've Got Troubles of My Own," "Tell Me, Dusky Maiden," "Mandy, Won't You Let Me Be Your Beau," "The Old Flag Never Touched the Ground," and "Oh, Didn't He Ramble." The income these songs brought was welcome, and the life was glamorous, on Broadway and on tours across the United States and in Europe; however, Johnson had serious reservations about such ephemeral work as genuine artistic expression. Reading Walt Whitman's *Leaves of Grass* (1855) in 1900, he became aware of the limitations of the dialect poetry he had been writing, depending as it did on white stereo-types of black life. Similarly, the vogue of coon songs on the musical stage ca-tered to racist attitudes. To achieve their popularity, Cole and Johnson Brothers had to work in this medium and to meet its expectations. Johnson managed to avoid the worst crudities of the genre, but in so doing he universalized his sub-jects by appealing to the bland sentimentalities of popular taste in love songs. At any rate, he had begun formulating plans for more serious literary work. In his spare time, he began a course of graduate study at Columbia University, espe-cially under the well-known critic Brander Matthews, who both respected his work in the popular theater and encouraged his more ambitious ventures.

Through the good offices of a political friend, Charles W. Anderson, John-son's career now took another turn, leading far away from New York. As the most influential black Republican in the city and a close friend of Booker T. Washington, Anderson exerted the leverage needed to secure Johnson a minor diplomatic post, that traditional sinecure for literary types. At the end of May 1906 Johnson arrived in Puerto Cabello, Venezuela, on the Caribbean, as United States Consul. Here he did indeed find time for his writing, producing numerous poems and making good progress on a novel. His next consular position, a slightly more desirable one in Corinto, Nicaragua, kept him busier dealing with business affairs, political unrest, and the revolution of (1906-1912). But in 1910 he took a furlough to marry Grace Nail, the cultivated daughter of a prosperous New York tavern owner and real estate dealer, and he also found time to com-plete the novel, *The Autobiography of an Ex-Colored Man* and to see it through the press. It was published anonymously by a small Boston house in 1912 while the author was still in Nicaragua.

The Autobiography of an Ex-Colored Man, tells the story of a light-skinned black man who finally crosses the color line and passes as white. Born in Geor-gia, the son of a prominent white man and his well-kept mistress, whose "skin was almost brown," he is moved, while still a small child, with his mother to Connecticut, where they are established in a comfortable cottage. The monthly checks sent from Georgia are supplemented by the mother's work as a seam-stress, making possible a genteel upbringing with a piano and books available in the home. But neither his quick mind nor his musical talent can shelter the boy from trauma when he discovers his racial identity through a humiliating episode at school. His father visits their home when the boy is twelve, but decreases his contact with his illicit family afterwards, not even responding several years later when the mother appeals to him in her last illness. She dies soon after her son's graduation from high school, leaving him quite alone in the world.

The protagonist's adult life drifts rather aimlessly. Returning to Georgia to matriculate at Atlanta University, he has his savings stolen on his second day in the city. Moving on to Jacksonville, he goes to work in a cigar factory and pre-pares to settle down and marry a schoolteacher. Instead, he is laid off and de-cides to go to New York, where he falls into the sporting life, becoming adept at gambling and playing ragtime music. Catching the fancy of a wealthy white man, he accompanies him to Europe, living first in Paris, then in Amsterdam and

Berlin. In the latter he finally forms a goal for his existence: he would voice all the joys and sorrows, the hopes and ambitions, of the American Negro, in classic musical form. Returning to the States, he disembarks in Boston, and, after sampling the life of the black middle class there, he travels south to Washington, Richmond, and Nashville. With Macon as a point of departure, he moves out into the Georgia hinterlands absorbing rural life, folk culture and its musical expression. Witnessing a lynching overwhelms him with racial shame, however, and he decides to return north and pass for white. Thoroughly emulating white values, he attends business college, gets a job, saves assiduously, and then speculates successfully in New York real estate. Marrying a white woman completes his transformation into "an ex-colored man," but at the end of the novel he realizes that he has "sold his birthright for a mess of pottage."

The Autobiography of an Ex-Colored Man is a novel, not an autobiography, but by issuing it anonymously Johnson hoped that it would be read as a true life story, giving it greater authenticity and impact than a work perceived as a mere piece of fiction. Certainly the protagonist is not Johnson himself, who could not pass and would not have wanted to. Nevertheless, the sources of the novel lie largely in Johnson's own experiences and friendships. His boyhood friend Judson Douglass Wetmore eventually passed and married two white women, the second a southerner. Like the protagonist of the novel, too, Wetmore became wealthy. On the other hand, many of the episodes parallel events in Johnson's own life. The Pilgrim's Progress and the Grimms' fairy tales were read by the novelist and his fictional character at a comparable age. Like his creator, the protagonist was disappointed in the drab backwardness of Atlanta, with its unpaved streets and lack of other urban amenities. Life in the Tenderloin district of New York attracted the protagonist as it had Johnson, who records his response in *Along This Way*: "an alluring world, a tempting world, world of greatly lessened restraints, a world of fascinating perils; but, above all, a world of tremendous artistic potentialities." (Johnson 11) In Paris the fictional character stays with his patron at the Hotel Continental and frequents a large cafe, where he improves his French by speaking with attractive young women. The author with his brother and Bob Cole stayed at the same hotel and worked on his French in the same way. Author and character responded to London as well as Paris in similar ways. Returning to the United States and traveling south, the protagonist encounters revival meetings like those Johnson attended as a child with his grandmother, even including an actual singing leader, "Singing Johnson", whom the writer was later to describe in his preface to *The Book of American Negro Spirituals* (1925). Most importantly, both Johnson and his fictional character were attracted to the riches of black folk expression and wished to make it available to a larger audience by rendering it in more artistic form.

From about the turn of the century Johnson had known the influential ally of Booker T. Washington, Charles W. Anderson, but he had known W.E.B. DuBois almost as long. In the summer of 1916 upon the invitation of Joel E. Spingarn and at the urging of DuBois, Johnson attended the important Amenia Conference on racial issues. A few months later he received from Spingarn an offer to become field secretary of the National Association of the Advancement of Colored People, which had been organized in 1910 by whites and blacks to provide a more militant vehicle for racial protest than Washington offered. Accepting the position in December, Johnson was to prove extremely effective in organizing local branches throughout the country, greatly expanding the membership of the organization. He also made an investigative trip to Haiti, exposing the abuses of American occupation of that country in a series of articles for the Nation in 1920. Later in the same year he became general secretary (the chief executive position) of the NAACP. Throughout the 1920s he provided effective leadership, aided by such subordinates as Walter White and William Pickens. Emphasizing legal action, publicity, and political pressure, Johnson coordinated the most effective movement against racism of its time. Even when he failed to win an immediate goal, as in the defeat of the Dyer Anti-Lynching Bill, he called the country's attention to the issue of racial injustice.

"I got immense satisfaction out of the work which was the main purpose of the National Association for the Advancement of Colored People," Johnson recalled in *Along This Way*: "at the same time, I struggled constantly not to permit that part of me which was artist to become entirely submerged." (Johnson 25). Official duties, including much travel and public speaking, occupied most of his time, but he managed to compile three important anthologies in the 1920s. (Johnson 25).

It is ironic that Johnson, an avowed agnostic, contributed so significantly to increased respect for the soulful richness of black Christianity. Before collecting spirituals, he has paid tribute in "O Black and Unknown Bards" to their creators. Religious themes appear elsewhere in his poetry, as in "Prayer at Sunrise" and in the untitled envoi to *Fifty Years and Other Poems*. But these are overshadowed by the superb achievement of *God's Trombones: Seven Negro Sermons in Verse*. The individual titles are "Listen, Lord-A Prayer," "The Creation," "The Prodigal Son," "Go Down Death-A Funeral Sermon," "Noah Built the Ark," "The Crucifixion," "Let My People Go," and "The Judgement Day." Two of the best of these, "The Creation" and "Go Down Death-A Funeral Sermon," had previously appeared in periodicals, the former in *The Freeman* in 1920. Johnson began work on "The Creation" after hearing a black preacher in Kansas City in 1918, but his interest in the poetic potential of the material preceded this occasion: "I had long been planning that at some time I should take the primitive stuff of the old-time Negro sermon and, through art-governed expression, make it into poetry. I felt that this primitive stuff could be used in a way similar to that in which a composer makes use of a folk theme in writing a major composition. I believed that the characteristic qualities: imagery, color, abandon, sonorous diction, syncopated rhythms, and native idioms, could be preserved and, at the same time, the composition as a whole be enlarged beyond the circumference of mere race and given universality." (Johnson, *Negro Americans, What Now?* vii).

Johnson's life came to an abrupt end on 26 June 1938, when he was killed in a car-train accident while traveling to his summer home in Maine. The accomplishments of his career, literary and otherwise, constitute a major and imperishable part of the history of Afro-American experience and expression in the early twentieth century.

The aforementioned literary Artists as Activists reflected in their writing, the growing race consciousness among African-Americans and the opposition to the segregation encountered in all forms of life. These writers have presented and understood the thought of African-American people who, though quite articulate in their own lifetimes, have been rendered historically inarticulate by the racist establishment. In the midst of the brutalities and injustices of the American racial system, these Artists as Activists during the Harlem Renaissance were able to find the means to sustain a far greater degree of self-pride and group cohesion than the system they lived under ever intended for them to be able to do. Upon the hard rock of racial, social and economic exploitation and injustice, these Artists forged and nurtured a culture.

During the same period the NAACP launched campaigns against lynching, the segregation of workers in the Civil Service, Jim Crow legislation in transportation, disfranchisement and residential segregation laws. The NAACP maintained that although Negroes demanded full citizenship both as a natural right and because America claimed to be a democracy, they would make themselves worthy of such rights-opportunity, not charity, was wanted and self-help was to continue.

The literary Artists as Activists during the Harlem Renaissance truly believed in helping themselves; given the kinds of social, economic, and political and physical abuse that African-Americans suffered from slavery through the Harlem Renaissance, it is inevitable that Black Writers as the voice of the masses would react in protest. C.W. Bigsby contends, "a protest expressed in varying degrees of intensity, but which is always at the root of creativity." (Bigsby 78)

For African-Americans have been subordinated, marginalized, positioned, and devalued in every possible manner to glorify and relentlessly hold in place the white-dominated symbolic order and racial hierarchy of American society. The Harlem Renaissance Writers were a group of freedom-seeking, socially conscious, politically active Artists. They demanded in their writings a larger role for African-Americans. These Artists as Activists were intellectuals, in terms of perceptions and illuminations, whose emergent cultural voices struggled to give critical and theoretical consciousness to this irrepressible, insurgent object of racism in American Society.

Harlem Renaissance Artists as Activists, sought a need to articulate the issue of African-American human rights, for greater emancipation and social justice.

The Harlem Commission reported that "among all classes, there was a feeling that the outburst of the populace was justified and that it represented a protest against discrimination." (The Negro in Harlem 11)

Unimpressed by the performance of this country under the dominance of white, Western culture, African-Americans   writers looked to their own cultural heritage as a source of affirmation of a different set of values. The exclusion of African-Americans from the mainstream of American culture has made rejection of that culture less difficult, for as James Baldwin suggests: "The American Negro has the great advantage of having never believed that collection of myths to which white Americans cling." (Baldwin 115). Many African-American writers questioned the cost involved in aiming for inclusion on terms which were irrevocably the terms of white culture. The thrust toward cultural assimilation became considerably weakened or reversed by these understandings. As Baldwin put it, "Do I really want to be integrated into a burning house?" (Baldwin 108)

Harlem Renaissance writers have frequently looked to Africa for recognition of common origins and culture, and the influence has been reciprocal. The dominant thrust of protest creating this Social Movement known as the Harlem Renaissance was toward political, social, economic and cultural inclusion into American institutions on a basis of full opportunity and full equality. Among the results were the landmark decisions in Shelly v. Kraemer, striking down restrictive covenants in housing, and the series of cases leading up to Brown v. Board of Education, declaring that the doctrine of "separate but equal" was inherently discriminatory in the public school   Frederick Douglass the father of Black Identity, Black Consciousness and Black Pride says it best, "Those who profess to favor freedom, and yet deprecate agitation, are men who want crops without plowing up the ground." (Douglass 218)

PROTEST, BURKEIAN ANALYSIS

The protest rhetoric of Jessie Fauset symbolizes a self reliant, independent and sophisticated African American Woman. Fauset's rhetoric was a symbol of racial pride and identity. As published in *Communication Quarterly*, in "Dramatism As Ontology or Epistemology", Kenneth Burke indicates, " Dramatism is an ontological system which offers literal statements regarding the nature of the human being as a symbol user and the nature of language as an act." (Brock, Burke, Burgess, Simons: Winter, 1985, 17)

Roi Ottley, in his book, *Black Odyssey*, contends, "*There is Confusion*, Jessie Fauset wrote of the beauty, sophistication and indeed the snobbery of Negro society." (Ottley 254)

The African American reaction to white prejudice and violence that sparked the Harlem Renaissance, forced intellectuals in the ghettos of the North to question their race, their environment and their nation.

Jessie Fauset and James Weldon Johnson created their art as a form of self expression. These artists created a definitive form of presentation of the artistic and social goals of the New Negro Movement known as the Harlem Renaissance.

As published in *Communication Quarterly*, in "Epistemology and Ontology as Dialectical Modes in the Writings of Kenneth Burke", James Chesebro purports, "Thus, as originally cast dramatism was to function as a practical art, explaining persuasion and self-expression." (Chesebro 179)

James Weldon Johnson in his autobiography, *Along This Way*, summed up the plight of the Negro and the need for self-expression. "The Negro's civil status had fallen until it was lower than it had been at any time since the Civil War; and, without noticeable protest from any part of the country." (158)

James Chesebro continues, "The Dramatistic theory of symbol-using deals with universals of the human condition and universals of communication." (Chesebro 181)

James Weldon Johnson provided effective group leadership as the Chief executive of the NAACP during the 1920s. Johnson drafted resolutions that demanded the end of lynching, the repeal of segregation, the abolition of Jim Crow and equal civil rights in public institutions.

Chesebro explains, "Burke's theory of symbol-using seeks to explain how different kinds of rhetorical systems are created and sustained by specific groups of agents." (Chesebro 181)

Jessie Fauset and James Weldon Johnson as rhetorical agents of the Harlem Renaissance gave the scene, its dramatism, its symbols of oppression, as seen through their writings.

Chesebro further explains. "law functions as a rhetorical system which creates, maintains and alters certain human norms during a particular era or specific time and place. (Chesebro 181)

The Minstrel, The Coon are seen as funny men by white America in a very stereotypical fashion. However, in her essay, "The Gift of Laughter", Jessie Fauset looks at this type of characterization as demeaning. Fauset's essay is published in the 1925 edition of *The New Negro* by Alain Locke. Fauset argues, "the black actor has been presented to the world as the "funny man" of America. Blacking their faces, presented the antics of plantation hands under the caption of "Georgia Minstrels."(Fauset 161) This vehement essay shows how Fauset feels the negative image of blackface minstrels is a racial stereotype of inferiority.

Kenneth Burke indicates in his article, "A Dramatistic View Of The Origins of Language", published in *The Quarterly Journal of Speech*, that the, "negative is a peculiarly linguistic resource, language adds the peculiar possibility of the negative. We would say that the negative must have begun as a rhetorical or hortatory function." (Burke 251)

James Weldon Johnson was the author of the Negro National Anthem, "Lift Every Voice and Sing", this was a song of hope, faith and courage for all African Americans. This song was an inspiration to fight for freedom against the odds. To march, protest and believe in the liberation of all Black people in the United States.

Johnson was truly a renaissance man of arts and letters. Johnson was versed in the classics and had an increasingly interdisciplinary mind. His work covers the fields of Music, Literature, Law, Education, Social Science, Foreign Languages(he was fluent in Spanish).

James Weldon Johnson who during a busy life found time to write many books, poems and articles, was the recognized guru of African American art and culture. He was a man of cultivation and great personal charm and he had the gift of inspiring writers, artists and musicians. He established his unique position with his *Book of American Negro Poetry*, an anthology published in 1922, which contained an astute critical evaluation of "The Negro Creative Genius". Already he had made a reputation in collaboration with his brother, J. Rosamond Johnson, writing songs for the light opera stage. This distinguished African American had a versatile career. He became contributing editor of the *New York Age*, a Black newspaper in Harlem. Meanwhile, he had written the English libretto of the Spanish Opera, Goyescas, which was produced at the Metropolitan Opera House in 1915.

According to Brown, Davis and Lee, "Johnson was a pioneer, serving as an interpreter of Negro artistic achievement and a stimulus to Negro writers." (The Negro Caravan 325)

Kenneth Burke argues, "philosophy evolves from the view that language is a strategic response to a situation. (Burke, *The Philosophy of Literary Form* 3)

James Weldon Johnson wrote an essay, "Harlem: The Culture Capital, published in *The New Negro* by Alain Locke. Johnson promulgates, "I believe that the Negro's advantages and opportunities are greater in Harlem than in any other place in the country, and that Harlem will become the intellectual, the cultural and the financial center for Negroes of the United States, and will exert a vital influence upon all Negro peoples." (Johnson 311)

James Weldon Johnson was truly a man of words and rhetoric. "The use of words by human agents to form attitudes or to induce actions in other human agents." Kenneth Burke makes this clear in his book, *A Rhetoric of Motives*, (41).

3
THE WORLD OF DANCE & MUSIC

KATHERINE DUNHAM

The New York daily papers of January 17, 1941 carried a piquant notice to the effect that the chief dancer in one of Broadway's current musical hits would lecture to the Anthropology Club of the Yale University Graduate School on the practical application of primitive materials to the theatre, demonstrating her discourse with the aid of 10 performers. The notice was no more striking than the combination of talents within this gifted African-American choreographer, and the career they have shaped for her. Katherine Dunham has danced her way from the pews of a Methodist Church, through the torrid mysteries of Haitian voodoo, santeria and primitive ceremonials in Jamaica, Martinique, Trinidad, to Sunday night concerts in New York ("Tropics" and "le Jazz Hot" the names she called her programs) which launched her toward Broadway stardom.

That meant incidentally dancing her way through hardship, discouragement, indefatigable labor, to success. Due to the racial segregation in American, she had to work extra hard. Her goal was suggested by the dictum of the *New York Herald Tribune's* critic, Walter Terry: "Katherine Dunham is laying the groundwork for a great Negro dance." (Terry 1)

She has mastered the steps and contortions that characterize Black dances from the plantation to the Harlem "joint"; has studied and reproduced the juba, the rumba, the danse du ventre, as well as the cakewalk and the shimmy. These become, however, not her performance but her raw material: elements to be fused and developed into an idiom of her own. It is never an "arty" idiom, and always expresses the vitality we associate with the dance and with the Negro. The same critic remarked that one feels "as if the performers (of her troup) were dancing because they felt an overpowering urge for rhythmic movement and not merely because they were scheduled to give a show." (Terry 2)

Miss Dunham's background contributed a number of elements to her diverse career. Her family was a pillar of the church in Joliet, Illinois, where she was born in 1910. Her mother , Annette Poindexter Dunham, was a school-teacher. Her father, Albert Millard Dunham, descended from Madagascar via Tennessee, kept a cleaning and dyeing establishment by day. At night he indulged a fondness for playing the mandolin and guitar, somewhat to the distress of Katherine and her brother Albert, who were commandeered to form a trio until Katherine openly revolted and Albert fled to the University of Chicago. Here he became one of the most brilliant students ever graduated from that institution. After taking his Master's at Harvard he returned to chicago for his Ph.D. and then went to teach at Howard University.

His little sister's education carried her to more distant and more exotic places, Her interest in the dance was evident even in Joliet, where at the age of eight she split the congregation wide open by staging a " cabaret party" to raise funds for the church. She cleared $32, which at the time seemed almost as much as the $2,000 her 1941 troupe took in weekly. Her parents did not worry too much about her twinkling feet, since she stood very well in her studies, was class poet and occasionally a paid contributor to *Child Life* Magazine. But by the time she entered the University of Chicago she knew that choreography was her field, and had determined to earn her way through college by forming a dancing school. The school was in a cold, drafty barn, and it took much movement and instruction to   save teacher and pupils from pneumonia. They shivered and sneezed through it without fatal results, and the teacher managed at the same time to win distinction as student in her college courses. More important, for present purposes, she discovered the study of anthropology, which made it legitimate and feasible to study primitive dances.

Through a staunch friend, who was one of the Easy Aces radio performers, she met Mark Turbyfill, a ballet dancer with the Chicago Opera Company, and they developed the idea of a Negro Ballet. Earl Delamarter, assistant director of the Chicago Symphony Orchestra, was enlisted, and the three established a Negro school of dance which staged its first public appearance in 1931, with a *Negro Rhapsody* at the Chicago Beaux Arts Ball.

The Katherine Dunham Dance Group made its way slowly, until a performance in an abandoned loft resulted in a Julius Rosenwald Foundation Fellowship which enabled Miss Dunham to study native dance, ritual and folklore in the Caribbean and in Brazil. The steps she had to master were no more intricate than her social role in communities where both Black and White elements eyed with suspicion a young woman who frequently disappeared into the bush for days on end and sometimes came back with the eggs and feathers of a voodoo ceremony sticking to her hair. In Port-au-Prince she was actually warned to leave. Instead she rented the biggest theatre the town afforded and announced a concert. Her audience came armed with epithets and ripe fruit; but all that was flung at her was a shower of "Lovely, lovely!", "How Artistic!" and a pitter-patter of applause. For she appeared in a long tulle dress sprinkled with rosebuds, pranced daintily through a bit of Debussy, followed it with a castanet-clicking a Spanish number and ended with a *Fire Dance*, at the close of which she released a flock of doves into the audience. In comparison to that dual feat of penetrating the inner circles of local aristocracy and native priesthood, her conquest of Broadway seems almost a minor achievement. She returned from her travels with a large repertoire of dances, quantities of authentic and illuminating films, and a store of inside information on primitive cults and customs that commanded the respect of anthropologists.

Although critics and audiences have been glowing in their praise of Miss Dunham's performance, she rather prides herself on a realization that she is not a great dancer. She feels her forte to be choreography, the planning and directing of dances, the training of dancers. (Terry 10) Those who rhapsodize over her own prowess may be to some extent confused between pleasure in the dance and in the dancer, for not the least of Katherine Dunham's gifts is beauty. Moreover she has the ability, partly executive, to achieve settings and costumes which further her choreographic and dramatic effects. She is less a singer than a dancer, yet her low voice, half singing, half speaking, greatly enhances certain of her numbers.

Off stage her voice is also low, and unusually pleasing. Always quiet and reserved, she has an unusual ability to express herself in words, written or spoken. Two of her articles on dancing in Martinique were published in *Esquire* in 1939, and she has written since then a plethora of manuscripts on Dance in Third World Cultures.

Critics feel that Miss Dunham's own name is quite enough to characterize an artist whose talent, intelligence and abounding vitality put it in her power to rank as a major figure not just in exotic dances from the Third World, but as a major figure on the American dance stage.

In her book, *Island Possessed*, Katherine Dunham gives a detailed description of her initiation into the Rada Dahomey cult of the Vaudun(Voodoo) In her account of the public dance following the initiation ordeal she states:

> I felt weightless like Nietzsche's dancer, but unlike that dancer, weighted, transparent but solid, belonging to myself but a part of everyone else. This must have been the "ecstatic union of one mind" of Indian philosophy, but with the fixed solidarity to the earth that all African dancing returns to, whether in assault upon the forces of nature or submission to gods. (Dunham vii)

Her experiences and reflections were codified into a system referred to as "Dunham technique," in which the dances she learned from Haitian peasants were broken down and reassembled into a series of movements suitable to stage performances in a Western cultural setting.

She informed her dance programs with her knowledge of the cultures she studied, as well as her deep aesthetic and social sensitivity; and her dance troup's performances electrified audiences around the world.

Returning dance to the heart of social living, in the late 60s Dunham opened a cultural arts program in East St. Louis, Illinois under the auspices of Southern Illinois University at Edwardsville. In her activities there she has applied her knowledge and expertise gained from her Haitian and other international backgrounds to develop a sense of the community's participation in a larger world order and a different cosmic scheme based on values derived from her cultural investigations. In so doing, she has drawn upon many traditions and she has imported artists and other cultural representatives from various countries: Brazil, Haiti, Senegal, Barbados, as well as from other areas and ethnic groups in the United States. Her programs have offered a variety of cultural resources and education, with dance as the focus. The dance classes have attracted young people who in the beginning came merely to watch; according to one former student, the dance classes attracted her "like a magnet," and this note was repeated by other former students. Dunham's aim was to overcome some of the destructive elements in the young people's deteriorating environment, through an exciting and compelling artistic vehicle. She brought in performers from her former dance troupe who helped her train and develop a cadre of young instructors to serve as teachers, role models and to interpret Dunham technique and philosophy to the community. These activities have continued as a self-generating process of initiating young East St. Louis into the Dunham tradition of the arts.

Because Dunham's life work drew upon the rituals of the Voodoo of Africa, she has a keen understanding of the public uses and effectiveness of ritual. One of her most lasting pieces of choreography- *Rites de Passage* is a distillation of rites of passage she has observed worldwide, but particularly African ritual. She has used collective ceremony in many settings in East St. Louis, including a dedicatory ceremony attended by officials, donors and the general public, at which her dancers performed. The Katherine Dunham museum in East St. Louis opened with a ribbon-cutting ceremony in which African drummers and dancers were an integral part of the proceedings.

Like a precious stone glistening in a pile of rocks, the Katherine Dunham Museum and Children's Workshop is somewhat conspicuous at the corner of Tenth Street and Pennsylvania Avenue, amid the poverty and blight of East St. Louis, Ill. In that way, it is a fitting tribute to its founding force. Katherine Dunham, the legendary dancer, choreographer, anthropologist and writer who in the 30s, 40s and 50s revolutionized modern dance with her own brand of ethnic flavored creations.

On the very day she arrived in the smoldering city across the Mississippi River from the more prosperous St. Louis, Mo., she was arrested because she protested the random arrest of young Black men. University officials criticized her for being friendly with "militant types" and suggested that she move to the Carbondale, Ill., campus. "I'm here now, and this is where I'll stay!" the strong-willed Miss Dunham announced. "There was something burning all the time in this city," she recalls, "and I decided to direct some of that energy into something useful." That "something useful" at first was the University's Performing Arts and Training Center and later her own museum and dance school. "We had a very hard time at first teaching young men to dance, because they thought it absurd," she says, "but when we brought in drummers from Africa and the Car-

ibbean and incorporated martial arts and lectures, a lot more interest developed."
(Beckford 11)

Miss Dunham is no longer able to dance as she did so well during her performing career. Her gait is slow and sometimes painful, and she walks with the
assistance of a cane. Still, she takes great pleasure and pride in overseeing
youngsters from the East St. Louis area as they learn and perform the Dunham
Technique. In a coach house behind the museum that is filled with artifacts and
costumes from former Katherine Dunham dance troupes, children ages six
through 12 come after school to take dance lessons. During Black History
Month, they perform for as many as 10,000 people at various school, civic and
charitable programs. Attired in Caribbean and African costumes, the young performers dance to the rhythms of "African drummers," the young male dance
students. The dance troupe also performs ballet, jazz and tap dance numbers.

Katherine Dunham has had a very positive impact on the predominantly
Black community of East St. Louis, a city of 50,000 that was virtually destroyed
by the riots of the 60's and then abandoned by many White residents and once-
prosperous businesses. Darryl Braddix, an East St. Louis fireman and former
dancer who is director of the dance workshop, credits Miss Dunham with rescu-
ing him from the streets. "If not for her, I would probably be in jail-or in hell,"
he says. Now 38, Braddix first met Miss Dunham when she lectured at SIU in
1967. He later took her on a guided tour of his burned-out city, during which
Braddix was arrested "for questioning." Later, when Miss Dunham inquired
about Braddix and complained about police brutality, she also was jailed. (Allen
54)

That Katherine Dunham would settle in East St. Louis is no surprise to
those who have followed the life and career of this talented and community-
conscious matriarch of Black dance. (For almost 50 years she has also lived in
Haiti and shared her art, love and economic resources with its people.) Miss
Dunham's greatest artistic contribution has been her influence on American
dance by introducing the world to authentic African and Caribbean dance forms
in a concert setting. She has also traveled the "star" route to Broadway productions, Hollywood films and television shows. Throughout her career, she
amazed and entertained her audiences with her resourcefulness and creativity.

After publishing her research findings, Miss Dunham wanted to dance-and
did. She organized a dance company and during the Depression worked with the
Work Projects Administration (WPA), where she met her husband of 45 years,
John Pratt, who designed most of the elaborate costumes characteristic of her
performances. In 1940, Miss Dunham made her off-Broadway debut in *Tropics*
and *Le Jazz Hot*. She also took her dance company to Hollywood, where she
appeared in or choreographed numerous films, including *Pardon My Sarong*,
Carnival of Rhythm, Stormy Weather, Casbah, Mambo and *Green Mansions*. In
1944, Miss Dunham established a dance school in New York City. Over the
years she influenced such students as Earth Kitt, Geoffrey Holder, Jose Ferrer,
Rita Moreno, Marlon Brando, Arthur Mitchell and Pearl Primus. She has also
written and published five books.

In 1983, Miss Dunham was among five distinguished artists honored at the Kennedy Center Honors Gala and a White House reception hosted by President and Mrs. Reagan. She also has been honored in Chicago with a two-day Katherine Dunham Retrospective Festival that featured lectures on the Dunham Technique as well as dance performances. And her life and art have been captured in several documentaries and television specials. Choreographer, Alvin Ailey worked with Miss Dunham to stage and film her major productions before his death.

Despite all the honors, Katherine Dunham's greatest joy comes not from the numerous accolades but from the East St. Louis youngsters who are learning much of her vast knowledge of dance. Her greatest accomplishment, she says, "is breaking through various social barriers." (Allen 55) As the Grand Diva of Dance, the Katherine Dunham Technique is more than just dance, it is a way of life. She has truly made a significant impact on the lives of many young African-American dancers of today.

PROTEST, BURKEIAN ANALYSIS

Katherine Dunham is credited with creating a unique form of African American dance and placing it on the level of art form. Dunham has a background as an anthropologist, she weaved the concepts of ritual and dance together from the African diaspora and created an exotic blend of performance art. According to Kenneth Burke in *Language as Symbolic Action*, "Man is the symbol-using (symbol-making, symbol-misusing) animal." (Burke 16) Katherine Dunham sought to create a totally new type of symbol via creative movement, as her contemporaries were Martha Graham, Charles Wideman, Doris Humpheries and Jose Limon. Dunham sought to create a style of dance from the African, West Indian and African American cultural experience.

Now 95 years old Katherine Dunham is the only living major artist of the Harlem Renaissance, her life is the stuff of legend. In the late 1920s Katherine moved to Chicago to join her brother in taking classes at the University of Chicago. She began to take dance classes and to perform in local theatres. Dunham opened her own dance studio called "Ballet Negre." At School she was greatly influenced by the work of cultural anthropologists and learned to see dance as a cultural symbol.

According to Kenneth Burke in his work, *The Philosophy of Literary Form*, "people assess the human situation and shape appropriate attitudes by constructing their conceptions of the world around them. These strategies or stylized answers are symbols that reflect attitude." (Burke 3).

While living with the Accompong Maroons, in standard ethnographic practice, Dunham kept a journal and recorded her daily observations and experiences. She had to first win over the trust and confidence of the people and in doing so she collected information on a group about whom much still remains unknown.

Dunham was inspired by her time in Jamaica, with a wide range of ideas for new choreography and a new technique which combined principles of ballet and modern dance with an Afro-Caribbean dance. She used this new technique, soon labeled the "Dunham Technique" as a participant in New York's celebrated "Negro Dance Evening," and as dance director of Chicago's Federal Theatre Project.

Dunham was a staunch civil rights activist, staging protests against segregation in public spaces in the US. One of her major triumphs was the successful staging of a suit against a Brazilian hotel which eventually prompted the Brazilian president to apologize and outlaw discrimination in public places. She once refused to sign a lucrative Hollywood studio contract when the producer indicated a desire to replace some of the darker skinned members of her repertoire.

Dunham was inspired by the work of anthropologists Robert Redfield and Melville Herskovits, who stressed the importance of the survival of African culture and ritual in understanding African American culture. In *Language As Symbolic Action*, Burke's dictum is "that a reflection of reality is also a selection and a deflection." (Burke 115)

Dunham was searching for a change, for something new, importantly for the development of African American modern dance, her field work began her investigations into a vocabulary of movement that would form the core of the Katherine Dunham Technique. What Dunham gave modern dance was a coherent lexicon of the African and Caribbean styles of movement-a flexible torso and spine, articulated pelvis and isolation of the limbs, a polyrhythmic strategy of moving—which she integrated with techniques of ballet and modern dance.

Dunham kept up her brand of political activism. Fighting segregation in hotels, restaurants and theaters, she filed lawsuits and made public condemnations. To an enthusiastic but all-white audience in the South, she made an after-performance speech, saying she could never play there again until it was integrated. Dunham was the first African American female to choreograph at the Metropolitan Opera, their new production of "Aida".

Dunham was moved by the civil rights struggle and outraged by deprivations in the ghettos of East St. Louis, an area she knew from her visiting professorships at Southern Illinois University in the 1960s, Dunham decided to take action. In his article, "Rhetorical Criticism: A Burkeian Approach Revisited," Bernard Brock says, "Burke clearly demonstrates his view that verbal symbols are meaningful acts from which motives can be derived, the relationship between symbols and action." (Brock 184) She opened the Performing Arts Training Center, a cultural program and school for the neighborhood children and youth, with programs in dance, drama, martial arts, and humanities

In February 1992, at the age of 82, Dunham again became the subject of international attention when she began a 47-day fast at her East S. Louis home. Because of her age, her involvement with Haiti, and the respect accorded her as an activist and artist, Dunham became the center of a movement that coalesced to protest the United States' deportations of Haitian boat-refugees fleeing to the U.S. after the military overthrow of Haiti's democratically elected President

Jean-Bertrand Aristide. She agreed to end her fast only after Aristide visited her and personally requested her to stop. Kenneth Burke in his book, *Attitudes Toward History*, indicates, "certain functions or relationships as either friendly or unfriendly." (Burke 3)

Boldness has characterized Dunham's life and career and she is still going strong. And, although she was not alone, Dunham is perhaps the best known and most influential pioneer of black dance. Her synthesis of scholarship and theatricality demonstrated, incontrovertibly and joyously, that African American and African Caribbean styles are related and powerful components of dance in America.

MARIAN ANDERSON

When Toscanini heard Marian Anderson sing he said: "A voice like hers comes once in a century." The 75,000 people who came to hear her before the Lincoln Memorial on Easter 1939-the greatest crowd since Lindbergh's triumphal homecoming-and the thousands who bought tickets for her concerts months in advance are heartily in agreement. December 1935, when she gave her first overwhelmingly successful recital in New York City, Marian Anderson has remained, in the judgment of many, "the world's greatest contralto." She has been applauded by audiences throughout the United States, and her tours abroad have taken her to numerous other countries of the world. In the course of a season she may give as many as sixty recitals, for which she draws upon her repertory of some two hundred songs. The recordings of the "consummate artist" include the works of Bach, Brahms, Handel, Saint-Saens, and Schubert, as well as Negro Spirituals.

Marian Anderson was born on February 27 in the Negro residential section of South Philadelphia. Her parents, who had two younger daughters, were of modest means-her father was an ice and coal dealer, and her mother a school teacher. After attending the local grade school, Marian Anderson became a student at the South Philadelphia High School, from which she was graduated at the age of eighteen. Her chief interest from her childhood years was music. At the age of six she was a member of the junior choir of the Union Baptist Church and had sung before the congregation in a duet. Two years later, it is told, she earned her first money as a singer-the remuneration was fifty cents. Later, in the church's senior choir, which she joined at thirteen, the young girl learned how to sing several musical parts, demonstrating then the wide range of her voice for which she was later to become famous. She also sang at high school events, and it was then that John Thomas Butler, a Philadelphia actor, arranged for an interview for her with voice teacher Mary S. Patterson. From Miss Patterson, Miss Anderson received her first training; gratuitously A benefit concert of the Philadelphia Choral Society, at which Miss Anderson was soloist, netted five hundred dollars for the young singer, money which enabled her to study for two years with Agnes Reifsneider, a leading contralto and teacher in Philadelphia. Meanwhile, Miss Anderson continued to earn small sums of money by singing at club meetings and similar events, and well-wishers made contributions toward her musical education. At the age of nineteen the singer auditioned for Giuseppe Boghetti, well-known voice teacher, who accepted her as a student. Under his tutelage she trained for a contest among unknown singers for the privilege of singing with the New York Philharmonic Orchestra at the Lewisohn Stadium in New York City. The result was that she was chosen from among three hundred competitors, and in August 1925 appeared as soloist at the outdoor concert, singing the aria "O Mio Fernando" from the Donizetti Opera *La Favorita*. She was well received and was immediately signed for an engagement with the Philadelphia Symphony Orchestra, then under the direction of Eugene Ormandy. Aside from this and invitations from various glee clubs, choirs, and Negro organizations, Miss Anderson received relatively few engagements, as she was a young Negro Artist. The next year she studied with Frank La Forge and then, on a scholarship granted by the National Association of Negro Musicians, she went to Europe for further training, particularly in languages. (Anderson 19)

In 1929 Marian Anderson returned to the United States for a recital at New York's Carnegie Hall. There she met with a moderate response, but subsequently she received a Julius Rosenwald Scholarship for study abroad. In 1933, she met a German concert manager who agreed to arrange a debut for her in Berlin, at a cost of five hundred dollars to the singer. This recital a success, he then arranged a series of six appearances. Not only were the six recitals successful, but her engagements had increased to fourteen before she left Scandinavia. For the next two years her engagements took her through the Continent, with command performances for the kings of Sweden and of Denmark; singing for Sibelius, who honored her by dedicating the song "Solitude" to her; and concluding with an engagement at the 1935 Mozarteum, in Salzburg, Austria. It was there that Toscanini heard her and made his famous statement, "A voice like hers is heard only once in a hundred years." (Anderson 20)

That same year S. Hurok, hearing Miss Anderson at a Paris recital, signed an exclusive contract with her for her American appearances. It guaranteed a specified number of concerts and a specified sum for the season. On December 31, 1935, the contralto made her Town Hall debut, managing to appear in spite of a fractured foot, caused by a fall on the ship which brought her to New York. The curtain was lowered at the end of each group of songs so that the audience did not know of her injury until the intermission, when the curtain lowerings were explained. By this time the audience was completely won by her singing. The reviewers were equally enthusiastic, Howard Taubman of the *New York Times* particularly so-he described her voice as "stunning," and "transcending"; and her projection of songs as "music-making that probed too deep for words." (Taubman 21) In a second New York Times review Olin Downes wrote of her as a "contralto of shining range and volume, managed with suppleness and grace." (Downes 47) Two additional concerts were given in New York City that season, both at Carnegie Hall before a capacity audience.

Thereafter Miss Anderson's reputation as an artist increased. In 1936 she toured Europe, Africa, and South America, was asked to sing at the White House, and during the 1937-38 season gave seventy recitals in the United States, described by her management as the "longest, most intensive tour in concert history for a singer." At this time she made her initial appearance in the concert halls of cities in the Southern States. The next season she gave seventy-five concerts in sixty cities. It was while arranging for an engagement in Washington, D.C. in 1939 that her manager was refused booking at Constitution Hall, the headquarters of the D.A.R. Protest against the racial discrimination came from leading musicians and public figures; and the action was climaxed by the resignation of Mrs. Eleanor Roosevelt from the D.A.R.. Within a few days Miss Anderson was offered the use of Lincoln Memorial by the Federal Government. There, on Easter 1939 she sang on the steps before an audience of approximately 75,000. (A mural depicting this event has been placed on a wall in the United States Department of the Interior.)

Since that time Miss Anderson has continued to give sixty recitals each season, appearing for at least two every year at capacity-filled Carnegie Hall, at outdoor summer recitals, and in most of the cities of the United States, including those of the South. Her regular European tours were canceled during the years of World War II, but in 1949 she resumed her visits to the Continent. In 1949, she completed her fourteenth annual concert tour of the United States. The recordings made by Miss Anderson are in constant demand-250,000 copies of one of them, her Schubert "Ave Maria" have been sold, reported *Newsweek*. She has recorded many of the songs of her recital programs-of Bach, Brahms, Handel, Haydn, Schumann, Schubert; of Mendelssohn, Massenet, Saint-Saens, Verdi and Rachmaninoff. Her renditions of Negro spirituals are also available. The contralto has sung over the radio, on the Telephone Hour. (Stevenson 25) In general, critical opinion of Miss Anderson's artistry has not changed greatly from the reception given it in 1935, nor has she declined in popular appeal. In 1945 when she repeated at a Carnegie Hall recital the program she had sung ten years before at her Town Hall debut, she was greeted by an enthusiastic audience. Reviewers have usually reported her "superlative musicianship and understand," the "sensitivity and finesse" with which she interprets varied selections of songs and arias, and the "imposing volume and proclamative firmness of texture" of her upper tones. (Stevenson 26) The *New York Herald Tribune* critic of her January 1950 concert at Carnegie Hall wrote that there was "innate warmth" in her higher tones, and her "personality, commanding presence and the impression she gives her listeners of being absorbed in each song were persuasive as usual." (Stevenson 27) Her programs are carefully balanced, including the vocal works of Bach and Beethoven, the German Lieder of Schubert, Brahms, and Strauss, several arias from the Italian operatic repertory, and concluding with a group of spirituals. Her devout demeanor on the stage is commended by the reviewers, the *New York Herald Tribune* critic finding it a reflection of her "humility," her "inwardness" and her "rare artistry." (Stevenson 28)

Miss Anderson has been described by Howard Taubman, writing in the *New York Times*, as a "tall, stately woman, with an abundance of graciousness and good humor." *Time* wrote of her as a "dedicated character, devoutly simple, calm, religious"; she is reported to have said: "I do a great deal of praying." At a 1949 interview with *Newsweek* she was asked whether she had noticed any relaxing in Southern cities on the question of racial discrimination. She answered: "In some places the improvement is slower than in others, but there is evidence of a desire to take steps in the right direction." (Stevenson 29) In cities where there is segregation, she demands "vertical" seating. This means that Negro ticket purchasers, though seated apart from others, must be allotted seats in every part of the auditorium.

When not on tour Miss Anderson lives on her 105 acre farm near Danbury, Connecticut, with her husband, Orpheus H. Fisher, an architect of Wilmington, Delaware, to whom she was married in July 1943. There in her studio, with the aid of a recording system and Franz Rupp, her accompanist since 1941, she prepares four or five complete programs each year. In July 1939 she was awarded the Spingarn Medal, given annually to the American Negro who "shall have made the highest achievement...in any honorable field of endeavor." (Stevenson 30) The 1940 Bok award, given each year to an outstanding Philadelphia citizen, was presented to Miss Anderson in March 1941. Its accompanying prize of $10,000 became the basis of a Marian Anderson Award, administered by three trustees and used to help young people, without regard to race, creed, or color, to pursue an artistic career.

Marian Anderson has received honorary degrees of Doctor of Music from Howard University, Temple University, and Smith College. She is a member of Alpha Kappa Alpha, Sorority, Inc. Miss Anderson's habit of referring to herself in the first person plural when speaking of her singing has been attributed to "the humility with which she has always approached her great gift of song, and to the fact that she looks upon her accompanist as a full partner" "There was a time when I was very much interested in applause and the lovely things they said," she says. "But now we are interested in singing so that somebody in the audience will leave feeling a little better than when they came."(Newman 17)

Her repertoire was varied-two hundred songs in nine languages, Purcell and spirituals. No program of hers was complete without spirituals. "They are my own music," she says, "but it is not for that reason that I love to sing them. I love the spirituals because they are truly spiritual in quality; they give forth an aura of faith, simplicity, humility and hope." (Newman 18)

The success of Marian Anderson represents the triumph of genius over the greatest single obstacle an artist can be called upon to hurdle: race prejudice. There have been excellent Negro musicians before Anderson, and comparatively successful ones, too. But none, not even so sensitive an artist as Roland Hayes, has risen so high as she. To call Marian Anderson the greatest living Negro musician, as so many have done, is to qualify her reputation unwarrantably. She is more than that: She is one of the great artist of our century regardless of race, color or nationality. And, in some respects, she stands alone, majestic, incomparable.

Both as artist and as human being, she holds a regal position in music with rare stateliness. In her art, she has ever clung tenaciously to the highest standards alone; one can go through her career with microscopic thoroughness without discovering any hint of concession to expediency. So, in her everyday life, she has always behaved with rare integrity and dignity. I do not refer to her many benefactions to her race, which she prefers to keep unpublicized; I refer rather to the noble spirit and the beautiful pride with which, throughout her life, she has walked, in spite of the prejudice, the hatred, the ignorance surrounding her.

She has never descended to the level of those who have been hostile because of their color; on the contrary, she has always worn her color as a medal of honor. It is her practice to include at least one group of Negro Spirituals in every program, not because it is expected of her, but because it is the music of her race, the eloquent and poignant voice of her people. It is also her practice, when she appears on the stage of any concert hall that segregates Negroes, to bow to her own people first, and only afterwards to the rest of the audience. She does this simply, unostentatiously, almost with humility-telling the world that she cannot forget that she is a Negro, only because the world refuses to let her race forget its color.

Her rendition of Negro spirituals is, of course a deeply personal expression. To these songs she brings the full tragedy of a race despised and rejected. "Nobody Knows de Trouble I've Seen"-the expression of sorrow becomes more poignant and heartbreaking because of the restraint with which she speaks her woe. "Were You There When They Crucified My Lord?" -she brings the immense and shattering sorrow of one who knows what it means to be crucified. "Deep River"- with those unequaled low tones of hers, luscious in texture, the melody acquires wings and soars as never before.

On April 8, 1993 Marian Anderson died of congestive heart failure in Portland, Oregon, she was 96. As a great internationally acclaimed contralto, Marian Anderson helped break down racial barriers in the arts, after struggling to build a career in the U.S., she toured the world to universal praise.

PROTEST, BURKEIAN ANALYSIS

Many African American operatic and concert singers, including Leontyne Price and Kathleen Battle, have credited Marian Anderson as their inspiration. Price recalled the first recording she heard of the contralto: "I listened, thinking, this is beautiful, it was a revelation. And I wept." (Kozinn 20)

Anderson faced overt racism for the first time when she tried to apply for admission to a local music school. She recalled her reaction to the admissions clerk's racial comments:

"I don't think I said a word. I just looked at this girl and was shocked that such words could come from one so young."(Anderson, *My Lord What A Morning*, 57) In a 1952 article, "A Dramatistic View of the Origins of Language", published in *QJS*, Burke denotes, "the negative in language has probably developed through the negative command, "Do not do that." (Burke 253)

Although many concert opportunities were closed to her because of her race, she appeared with the Philadelphia Symphony and toured African American Southern College campuses. She made her European debut in Berlin in 1930 and made high successful European tours in 1930-32, 1933-34 and 1934-35. Still relatively unknown in the United States, she received scholarships to study abroad and appeared before the monarchs of Sweden, Norway, Denmark, and England. Her pure vocal quality, richness of tone, and tremendous range made her, in the opinion of many, the world's greatest contralto.

In 1939, however, she attempted to rent concert facilities in Washington's Constitution Hall, owned by the DAR, Daughters of the American Revolution, but was refused because of her race. Bernard Brock interprets Burke, "Language enables people to accept or reject their hierarchical positions or even the hierarchy; itself. Acceptance results in satisfaction and order, whereas rejection results in alienation and disorder."(Brock 185) This sparked widespread protest from many people, including Eleanor Roosevelt, who, along with many other prominent women, resigned from the DAR. Arrangements were made for Anderson to appear instead at the Lincoln Memorial on Easter Sunday, and she drew an audience of 75,00. On January 7, 1955, she became the first African American singer to perform as a member of the Metropolitan Opera in New York City. Before she began to sing her role of Ulrica in Verdi's *Un Ballo In Maschera*, she was given a standing ovation by the audience.

"The concept of acceptance follows from a positive reaction to the human situation" Brock argues in, "Rhetorical Criticism: A Burkeian Approach Revisited," (Brock 185)

In 1957 Anderson autobiography, *My Lord, What A Morning*, was published. The same year she made a 12 nation, 35,000-mile tour sponsored by the Department of State, the American National Theatre and Academy, and Edward R. Murrow's television series "See It Now." Her role as a goodwill ambassador for the United States was formalized in September 1958 when she was made a delegate to the United Nations. Anderson was awarded the Presidential Medal of Freedom by President Lyndon B. Johnson, and she was the recipient of numerous honorary degrees. Among her myriad honors and awards were the National Medal of Arts, Grammy Award for Lifetime Achievement and The Kennedy Center Honors. Although Marian Anderson faced racial prejudice throughout her career, she overcame it through perseverance.

Like Marian Anderson, the artists during the Harlem Renaissance had a dream that took much determination to make a reality. Anderson and the other artists during the Harlem Renaissance made their dream come true despite challenges and barriers of oppression, marginalization and vilification.

4
THE WORLD OF THEATRE & FILM

PAUL ROBESON

At the peak of his celebrity, while starring in Othello on Broadway, the immensely popular black actor, singer, and political activist Paul Robeson was the guest of honor of a birthday party given in April 1944 by the New York theatre world and an organization called the Council on African Affairs. So well-liked was Robeson that the celebration had to be held at the 17th Regiment Armory on Park Avenue to accommodate the nearly 8,000 guests. The sponsors of the tribute included some of the most famous names in show business as well as several prominent figures from the black community and the American left. By the end of the 1940's, with the Cold War in full swing and McCarthyism flourishing, such a gathering would have been highly unlikely. As the American political climate changed, however, Robeson clung to his admiration of the Soviet Union and to his denunciation of racial injustice. His commitment to views then considered radical and even subversive cost him his passport from 1950 to 1958 and, although he later made concert tours of Australia and Europe, cut short his career as one of America's most eloquent singers and actors.

Paul Leroy Bustill Robeson was born on April 9, 1898 in Princeton, New Jersey, the youngest of eight children of William Drew and Anna Louisa (Bustill) Robeson. After escaping from slavery at the age of fifteen, his father had changed his name from Roberson, the surname of his former owner, to Robeson. He joined the Union Army in 1861 and later worked his way through Lincoln University to become a Protestant minister. Paul Robeson's mother was a school-teacher of African, Indian, and English ancestry. When the boy was six years old, she died of burns in a household accident. Paul, the only child still at home, and his father, who had lost his Princeton ministry, moved to Westfield, New Jersey, and then to Somerville in the same state, where the Reverend Robeson became pastor of the St. Thomas African Methodist Episcopal Zion Church.

Shortly before his graduation from high school in Somerville in 1915, Paul Robeson scored highest in a competitive examination for a four-year scholarship to Rutgers College. The following fall he became the first of his family to enroll in a white college. At Rutgers he was the only black student and only the third black student in the school's history. Despite his racial isolation, he was very popular with his classmates. Standing six feet three inches tall and weighing 240 pounds as a young man, Robeson was described as "massive, beautiful in physique, muscular, strong and handsome," (Duberman 4) His deep voice and physical presence, then and later, impressed all who met him. He won the freshman prize for oratory and the sophomore and junior prizes for extemporaneous speaking. He earned twelve varsity letters in four sports-football, baseball, basketball, and track-and was named an All-American end in 1917 and 1918, winning the admiration of white teammates who had originally threatened a boycott if he were allowed to play on the football team. He served on the student council, gave the commencement address, and was elected to Phi Beta Kappa in his junior year and also to the Cap and Skull honor society. During all that time, Paul, like the other Robeson children, helped to support his college education by working at menial jobs in the summer.

When he left Rutgers with his B.A. degree in 1919, Robeson took an apartment in Harlem, where his reputation as an up-and-coming black youth had preceded him. In 1920 he entered the Columbia University Law School for training that he financed by playing professional football weekends. While in his first year at Columbia he agreed to perform in an amateur production of the play *Simon the Cyrenian* at the Harlem YMCA. He made his professional debut in 1921 in a presentation of the same play at the Lafayette Theatre.

For guidance in launching a career as an actor Robeson was primarily indebted to Eslanda Cardozo Goode, a chemistry student at Columbia whom he married on August 17, 1921. Having helped to persuade him to appear in *Simon*, she encouraged him to take time off from his studies to perform the starring role of Jim in *Taboo*, which ran on Braodway in 1922. Later in the year, renamed *Voodoo*, it was presented in Blackpool, England, with Robeson playing opposite Mrs. Patrick Campbell. His trip to England, where he and his wife were able to travel without the hindrance of Jim Crow laws and racial prejudice, began a lifelong love affair with Great Britain and the Continent.

In 1923 Robeson graduated from Columbia with an LL.B. degree, was admitted to the New York bar, and was taken into a law firm headed by a prominent Rutgers graduate. His lack of enthusiasm for the limited opportunities open to him in law along with his feeling that white clerks resented a black giant in the office combined to shorten his career as a lawyer. He was moreover, tempted to return to the theatre by several members of the Provincetown Players-an experimental Greenwich Village company with which Eugene O'Neill was associated-who had seen his portrayal of "Simon the Cyrenian." During May 1924 Robeson starred at the Provincetown Playhouse in two O'Neill plays, in *The Emperor Jones* as Brutus Jones, the black dictator of a West Indian island, and in *All God's Chillun Got Wings*, a bold drama about an interracial marriage. Among those impressed by Robeson's apparently intuitive grasp of acting was the theatre critic George Jean Nathan who commented in the *American Mercury* (July 1924) that he "does things beautifully, with his voice, his features, his hands, his whole somewhat ungainly body, yet I doubt that he knows how he does them." (Layton 47) Brutus Jones was the role in which Robeson made his triumphal London debut in September 1925.

Earlier in 1925 Robeson had worked up a concert act with his friend, the pianist and composer Lawrence Brown. Their sellout concert in New York in April was so successful that they were signed to a 1925-26 concert tour, playing and singing Negro spirituals and folk songs in the United States, Great Britain, and Europe. Robeson's voice, a deep and stirring baritone, soon became familiar all over the world. He had always had an aptitude for languages, and now he studied them so that he could sing folk songs of several nations. He eventually mastered over twenty languages, including Chinese, Gaelic, and several African tongues. During the next fifteen years, he made over 300 recordings, sang on the radio, and gave concert tours with appearances on the stage and in films and eventually accumulated a large income. (Layton 48)

A few of his dramatic roles gave Robeson the opportunity to sing as well as act, such as the title character in *Black Boy*, which had a short run in New York in October 1926. As Joe in *Show Boat* he Sang "Ol' Man River" at the Drury Lane in London in 1928 and at the Casino in New York in 1930-. For British audiences he also portrayed Robert Smith (Yank) in *The Hairy Ape* (1931), Balu in *Basilik* (1935), the Workman and Lonnie in *Stevedore* (1936), and Toussaint in *Toussaint L'Overture* (1936). In New York in early 1940 he created the title role in *John Henry*, a play with music but little dramatic force.

The role for which Robeson won highest critical tribute was Othello, which he first played in London in May 1930. When the same production of Shakespeare's play, staged by Margaret Webster, opened at the Shubert Theatre in New York on October 19, 1943, Robeson drew uniformly ecstatic notices for his illuminating interpretation of the passionate and tragic Moor. The play made theatre history on two counts; it was the first *Othello* on Broadway with a black hero and a white supporting cast (Jose Ferrer and Uta Hagen); its run of 296 performances exceeded that of any previous Shakespearean drama on Broadway. A coast-to-coast tour followed its New York presentation. Robeson's performance in *Othello* at Stratford-on-Avon in 1959 was also hailed as magnificent. (Layton 49)

Two of the eleven motion pictures in which Robeson had leading or featured roles were film versions of plays in which he had appeared on the stage: *The Emperor Jones* (United Artists, 1933) and *Show Boat* (Universal, 1936). He played Basambo, an African chief, in *Sanders of the River* (United Artists, 1935); Umbopas, chief of another African tribe, in *King Solomon's Mines* (Gaumont British, 1937); a black American dock worker in *Song of Freedom* (Treo Productions, 1938); and a coal miner in Wales in *Proud Valley* (Supreme, 1941). Among his other films were *Dark Sands* (Record, 1938) and *Tales of Manhattan* (Fox, 1942). *In Native Land* (Frontier Films, 1942), a documentary based on a Senate investigation of discrimination in the South, he spoke the commentary and sang the musical score. Sidney Poitier once said of Robeson, "Before him, no black man or woman had been portrayed in American movies as anything but a racist stereotype." But Robeson felt he had not attained his goal. "I thought I could do something for the Negro race in films," he explained when he decided to give up working in motion pictures. "...The industry is not prepared to permit me to portray the life or express the living interests, hopes, and aspirations of the struggling people from whom I come." (Murray 126)

Over the years Robeson had acquire many interests and many friends beyond the entertainment business, becoming identified-and identifying himself-with left-wing causes. On his trip to the Soviet Union in 1934, he had been greatly impressed by the social experimentation he saw there. Revisiting that country often, he learned the Russian language and became as well known in Moscow as he was in London and New York. He once declared that Russia was the country he loved more than any other, and he sent his only child, Paul Jr., to school there, hoping that the absence of racial and class discrimination that Robeson believed was characteristic of Russia's schools would be to the boy's benefit.

During the 1930s Robeson spent much time in England, where he was asked to give benefit performances for Jewish and other refugees from Fascist countries. He readily agreed and gained entree into British left-wing circles. Here he made the acquaintance of the young men of the West African Political Union, among them Jomo Kenyatta and Kwame Nkrumah. In the midst of the Spanish Civil War he went to Spain to entertain Republican troops.

By the time the Robeson family returned to the United States, in 1939, to make America their home again, the Roosevelt years had wrought a perceptible change in the country's racial climate, and Robeson found it a more congenial place than the land he had left in 1928. He recorded a patriotic song called "Ballad for Americans," which became an instant hit and seemed to articulate the people's renewed faith in the vigor of the country and its democratic ideals.

Both Robesons considered themselves dedicated participants in what Paul Robeson once called "the struggle against anti-Semitism and against injustices to all minority groups." He joined organizations like the Joint Anti-Fascist Refugee Committee, the Committee To Aid China, and the National Maritime Union, which made him an honorary member. His reputation as an entertainer was now fused with a new identification as a spokesman for the oppressed. That was no problem during World War II, when the "popular front against Fascism" was official United States policy. But in the late 1940's, as the Cold War intensified, Robeson began to suffer the same disrepute as thousands of other Americans with similar convictions.

Called before a committee of the California State Legislature in 1946, Robeson testified that he had never been a member of the Communist party, but after that experience he refused to answer such questions, on principle. The House Committee on Un-American Activities routinely cited him in those days as a "Communist" or "Communist sympathizer," and people began to pay attention. Demands were made at Rutgers University that Robeson's name be removed from the alumni rolls and athletic records and that an honorary degree given Robeson earlier be rescinded. His recordings were withdrawn from stores and he was often denounced in newspaper editorials, In other words, Robeson was "black balled" by McCarthy and the racist American establishment. (Robeson 24)

As the government and the public began to turn against him, Paul Robeson reaffirmed his views on the Soviet Union with increased vigor. In 1949 he made a controversial statement to the World Peace Congress in Paris:

> It is unthinkable that American Negroes could go to war on behalf of those who have oppressed us for generations against a country (the Soviet Union) which in one generation has raised our people to the full dignity of mankind." (Robeson 25) Aside from feeling affection for the Russian people, who had warmly received him on so many occasions, Robeson had come to embrace "scientific socialism," as he wrote in his autobiographical *Here I Stand*: "On many occasions I have expressed my belief in the principles of scientific socialism, my deep conviction that for all mankind a socialist society represents an advance to a higher stage of life." (Robeson 10)

The unpopularity of Robeson's views in a country grown increasingly fearful of Communism erupted in riots in the town of Peekskill, New York in August 1949, when several liberal and radical groups held a music festival at which Paul Robeson was the featured attraction. Although Robeson finally managed to sing, over 100 concertgoers were injured. The experience angered and saddened him, and only confirmed his belief that America was becoming a reactionary nation.

In 1950 the State Department demanded that Robeson surrender his passport and refused to issue a new one until he signed a non-Communist oath and promised not to give political speeches while abroad. Robeson's unwillingness to comply led to a long and frustrating battle through the federal courts that did not end until 1958, when the Supreme Court in a similar case found the government's actions unconstitutional. During those years Robeson was virtually prevented from earning a living, because the only concerts open to him in the United States were before small radical groups. In 1952 the Soviet Union awarded Robeson the Stalin Peace Prize, certainly a tribute that did nothing to alleviate his troubles at home.

By the time Robeson recovered his passport, which was revoked by the U.S. Government, the public's feelings about Communism had cooled somewhat, and in 1958 he gave a farewell concert at Carnegie Hall in New York, his first appearance there in eleven years. He made a short tour of the West Coast, recorded an album, and then left the United States, remaining abroad (London, Europe, Moscow) until 1963. While in Russia in 1959, Robeson became ill and was hospitalized. From then until his return to America he was in and out of hospitals and nursing homes in Moscow, Eastern Europe, and London, suffering from exhaustion and from a circulatory ailment. In 1963 Robeson and his wife returned to the United States amid rumors, denied by Eslanda Robeson, that he had become disenchanted with Marxism. He would not speak to the press, however, except to announce his retirement from the stage and from all public affairs, and he went into a seclusion. After the death of Eslanda Robeson in December 1965, Paul Robeson was able to keep his home only for a short time in New York City on Jumel Terrace, where his son and two grandchildren visited him. He eventually moved to Philadelphia to be with his sister, Mrs. Marion Forsythe.

The rich, powerful voice of Paul Robeson continued to be heard in recordings, such as the album *Songs of My People*, RCA victor's 1972 selection of spirituals and other songs taken from old discs made by Robeson and Brown in the 1920s. Also available in the early 1970s were Vanguard's three albums, *Paul Robeson at Carnegie Hall*, *Paul Robeson Recital*, and *Ballad for Americans*, as well as Columbia's album *Spirituals and Popular Favorites* and Odyssey's *Songs of Free Men*.

Robeson's name reappeared in the news in 1975, following reports, originating with his son, that he would like to be inaugurated into the National Football Foundation Hall of Fame. The movement was headed by Rutgers President, Dr. Edward J. Bloustein, who appealed to the foundation on behalf of Robeson, calling him "a brilliant scholar-athlete and brilliant artist in the finest tradition of collegiate higher education." (Gewen 18) He faced opposition, however, among directors of the foundation because of Robeson's political views and his long residence outside the country. In addition to the Stalin Peace Prize, Paul Robeson is the recipient of honorary degrees from Hamilton College and Rutgers University; the Spingarn Medal of the NAACP; the Whitney Young Jr. Memorial Award of the New York Urban League; and the Donaldson Award for the best acting performance of 1944 for his role as Othello.

On April 15, 1973 a "75th Birthday Salute to Paul Robeson" was organized at Carnegie Hall by leaders in the entertainment world and the civil rights movement, among them Harry Belafonte, Sidney Poitier, Zero Mostel, Coretta Scott King, and Angela Davis. Mrs. King paid tribute to Robeson for tapping "the same wells of latent militancy" among blacks that Martin Luther King, Jr., had inspired. Robeson was too ill to attend the celebration, but he sent a tape-recorded message in which he said, "I want you to know that I am still the same Paul, dedicated as ever to the worldwide cause of humanity for freedom, peace and brotherhood." (Gewen 18)

Robeson championed the cause of the oppressed throughout his life, insisting that as an ARTIST he had no choice but to be an ACTIVIST. Robeson died on January 23, 1976 after years of failing health, he spent the last 13 years of his life in self-imposed seclusion. Robeson and his good friend Marian Anderson were considered gifted and talented, high on the list amongst the most distinguished Americans (white or black) of the 20th Century.

PROTEST, BURKEIAN ANALYSIS

Paul Robeson was the epitome of the 20th-century Renaissance man. He was an exceptional athlete, actor, singer, cultural scholar, author, and political activist. His talents made him a revered man of his time, yet his radical political beliefs all but erased him from popular history. Today, more than one hundred years after his birth, Robeson is just beginning to receive the credit he is due.

Paul Robeson's areas of allegiance and political alignment were fused with broader cultural elements. Thus, racial strife caused Robeson increasing exclusion. Kenneth Burke in his book, *Attitudes Toward History*, states, "rejection is simply a shift in the allegiance to some other symbols of authority." (Burke 21)

Returning to his love of public speaking, Robeson began to find work as an actor. With songs such as his trademark "Ol Man River," he became one of the most popular concert singers of his time. His "Othello" was the longest-running Shakespeare play in Broadway history, running for nearly three hundred performances. It is still considered one of the great-American Shakespeare productions. While his fame grew in the United States, he became equally well-loved internationally. He spoke fifteen languages, and performed benefits throughout the world for causes of social justice. More than any other performer of his time, he believed that the famous have a responsibility to fight for justice and peace. In a time of deeply entrenched racism, he continually struggled for further understanding of cultural difference. At the height of his popularity, Robeson was a national symbol and a cultural leader in the war against fascism abroad and racism at home. Burke argues, "human beings are symbol users, metaphorical or literal? People really do act when linguistically identifying and distinguishing." (Burke 23)

Robeson's black nationalist and anti-colonialist activities brought him to the attention of Senator Joseph McCarthy. In *Permanence and Change,* Burke writes, "Bureaucracies-has its own hierarchy; and when two of these hierarchies are in conflict one will inevitably be rejected." (Burke 283) Despite his contributions as an entertainer to the Allied forces during World War II, Robeson was singled out as a major threat to American democracy. Every attempt was made to silence and discredit him, and his persecution reached a climax when his passport was revoked. He could no longer travel abroad to perform, and his career was stifled.

To this day, Paul Robeson's many accomplishments remain obscured by the propaganda of those who tirelessly dogged him throughout his life. His role in the history of civil rights and as a spokesperson for the oppressed of other nations remains relatively unknown. If we are to remember Paul Robeson for anything, it should be for the courage and the dignity with which he struggled for his own personal voice and for the rights of all people. Burke defines "frames of acceptance" as "the more or less organized system of meanings by which a thinking man gauges the historical situation and adopts a role relation to it." (Burke, *Attitudes Toward History* 5)

As citizens of the United States of America, we are guaranteed certain rights by the Constitution and the Bill of Rights. When we practice these rights, such as the freedom of speech, we are protected under these documents. There are times, however, when individual rights may be limited or denied by the actions of the government, other people, or by circumstance. "The West Virginia Library Commission has removed a biography of Paul Robeson, Negro singer, from its list of books recommended for children." (*New York Times.* 12 March 1948) Caption: "Enters Motion Against Robeson" The denim trouser-clad girl in the foreground puts the finger on her feelings about the Paul Robeson concert near Peekskill, N.Y., Sunday as a state trooper hold in check a group of men and women taking part in a demonstration against the singer. Veterans and their supporters paraded past the concert grounds as nearly 1,500 peace officers tried to keep them from clashing with the audience. (Photograph from *Morning World Herald, Omaha.* 5 September 1949)

Robeson took the position that he would no longer sing at concerts where audiences were segregated. Kenneth Joel, a graduate of Rutgers College, Class of 1942, was present at a Robeson concert in Kansas City, Missouri when he witnessed Robeson's refusal to perform in front of a racially segregated audience.

In *The Rhetoric of Religion*, Burke presents this concept which truly is at the crux of Robeson and the race problems he faced during his life, "Redemption need Redeemer (which is to say, a Victim!) To Victimage (hence: Cult of the Kill)..." (Burke 4)

Oscar Micheaux

Oscar Micheaux was a fiercely independent promoter of his own novels and films. He often involved his leading characters in personal and financial struggles for success that mirrored experiences central to his own life. An ardent supporter of the doctrines of Booker T. Washington, who urged that blacks set their own condition through diligence and dedication to practical goals, Micheaux conceived of his work as inspirational as well as entertaining.

Micheaux stands apart from his contemporaries in black letters. In his early books, Micheaux did not write of the rural South, as did Charles W. Chesnutt and Paul Laurence Dunbar, nor of northern ghettos, as did James Weldon Johnson. Nor do his early books focus, as did much black fiction of the period, on the tragic results of slavery and the problems resulting from the powerlessness of blacks in American society. His later novels show that he was but influenced by the Harlem Renaissance; he returns instead to the fictive techniques of his youth.

Undoubtedly the most successful of all black-owned independent film production companies which produced films about black people and employed all-black casts was the Micheaux Film and Book Corporation, which later became the Micheaux Film Corporation. This company, founded in 1918, was the only black-owned company which continued to produce films through the 1920s and 1930s. This company was established by one of the most colorful characters in the history of American films, Oscar Micheaux. During the 21 years between 1918 and 1940, Micheaux produced and distributed nationally and in Europe over 30 black-cast films, many of which were based on books which he wrote himself. Until recently, Micheaux has received very little recognition by film historians, but among his contemporaries who knew him he was considered to be a skilled entrepreneur, an astute businessman and a man who was sensitive to the needs of the black film audience. From an analysis of the responses of black film audiences to his films, Micheaux concluded that they did not care for propaganda as much as they did for a good story. Although he recognized that a strong story line was a key ingredient for a successful film, Micheaux also felt that his films should depict accurately the social, economic and political conditions under which the black man existed in America. Although perhaps not intended as such, some of his films can be considered as protest films. They were, in any event, considered at the time, by both whites and blacks, to be quite controversial.

Micheaux was born in Metropolis, Illinois in 1884. Not much is known about his parents and early childhood, although it is known that he had a brother, Swan Emerson Micheaux. The extent of his formal education is uncertain, but in his youth he worked as a Pullman porter and a farmer. Later, as a young man, he was a rancher. In 1909, at the age of 25, Micheaux purchased a homestead in South Dakota and after five years had successfully expanded his holdings to 500 acres. (Jet 26)

During his period as a rancher in South Dakota, Micheaux conceived and wrote a book titled *The Homesteader* which he eventually published in 1914 or 1915. In 1915 he established the Western Book and Supply Company, headquartered in Sioux City, Iowa. Micheaux worked hard traveling about the countryside around Sioux City selling his book, primarily to white farmers and businessmen. *The Homesteader* was based on his experiences as a rancher and the characters in it were Negro substitutes for the white persons with whom he had been in contact. The book was fully illustrated and sold for $1.50 per copy. (Jet 27)

In 1918, Micheaux's book came to the attention of George P. Johnson, then General Booking Manager of the black-owned and operated Lincoln Film Company of Los Angeles, California. From his office in Omaha, Nebraska, Johnson contacted Micheaux regarding the feasibility of letting Lincoln Film Company produce *The Homesteader*. Micheaux responded favorably to this proposition and in May 1918 traveled to Omaha and lived in Johnson's house for two days while discussing the details of the contract. Eventually, contractual papers were drawn up and ready to be signed, but Micheaux insisted that as part of the agreement he would go to Los Angeles and supervise the filming of the story. On the basis of Micheaux's lack of film experience, Johnson and the other directors of the Lincoln Motion Picture Company decided that they could not go along with the deal, and hence it fell through. This is the set of circumstances that launched Oscar Micheaux into a career of film production.

In 1918, Micheaux organized the Micheaux Film and Book Company with offices in Sioux City and Chicago, Illinois to produce the film *The Homesteader*. Using his considerable skills as a businessman and salesman, Micheaux sold stock in his corporation to the white farmers around Sioux City at prices ranging from $75 to $100 per share. Eventually enough capital was secured to produce *The Homesteader* as an eight-reel film starring Charles Lucas as the male lead, and Evelyn Preer and Iris Hall, two well-known dramatic actresses who at the time were associated with the Lafayette Players Stock Company.

In 1920, Micheaux's brother Swan joined him as Manager of the Micheaux Film and Book Company. Swan was later promoted to Secretary and Treasurer and General Booking Manager. In 1921, in order to take advantage of better studio facilities and the availability of more talented actors, the company established an office in New York City. The distribution and financial office remained in Chicago under the supervision of Swan Micheaux and Charles Benson, formerly with the Quality Amusement Company. Tiffany Tolliver and W. R. Crowell, operating out of a branch office in Roanoke, Virginia, were in charge of the distribution of the company's films in the east. The distribution of films in the southwest was done by A. Odams, owner of the Verdun Theatre in Beaumont, Texas. Production of the film *DECEIT* was begun at the Estees Studios in New York, June 6, 1921. (Jet 28)

The first controversial film produced by Micheaux was *WITHIN OUR GATES* (1920), controversial because it contained a scene involving the lynching of a Negro in the south. The film was shown for the first time in Chicago at Hammon's Vendome Theatre. Before that, however, the picture had been turned down by the Chicago Board of Movie Censors because it was claimed that its effect on the minds of the audience would result in a race riot similar to the one which had occurred in Chicago a year earlier. The picture was given a second showing at the Censor Board, and a number of prominent people, including a representative of the Association of the Negro Press, were called in to see the picture and express their opinions on the effect the film might have on public sentiment.

Opinion was divided after the showing. Those who objected pointed out that because of the previous race riot, showing the film would be dangerous. Others who approved argued that because of the existing conditions of the time, the lynchings and handicaps of ignorance, it was time to bring such issues before the public. Among those who argued forcefully for the film were Alderman Louis B. Anderson and Corporation Counsel Edward H. Wright. These men, with the endorsement of the press, prevailed, and a permit to show the film was finally granted.

Those who objected, however, did not give up. They visited churches and protested at length against the showing. Among the most vigorous protesters were black, many of whom had not seen the picture. The protests against the film continued right up to the day of the opening of the film. That morning a committee was appointed from the Methodist Episcopal Ministers' Alliance, consisting of both whites and blacks. The committee visited the Mayor of Chicago and the Chief of Police, but without avail. The picture opened to a packed house.

WITHIN OUR GATES was shown at the Loyal Theatre in Omaha, Nebraska on August 9, 1920. It had taken two months to get approval from the Omaha Censor Board.

Many theaters in the south refused outright to book the film because of its "nasty story." The white manager of the Star Theatre in Shreveport, Louisiana, refused to book the picture on advice of the Superintendent of Police in New Orleans who stated that:

> ...the present Manager of the Temple Theatre stated that he had witnessed this picture demonstrating the treatment during slavery times with which the negroes were treated by their masters, also show the execution by hanging of about nine negroes for absolutely no cause and that it is a very dangerous picture to show in the south." (Bogle 31)

The controversy caused by *WITHIN OUR GATES* did not deter Micheaux from making another picture with a similar theme. He made *THE GUNSAULUS MYSTERY*, in 1921. This eight-reel film was based on a murder case in which Leo Frank was convicted of a the crime. The movie was filmed in New York Studios and starred Evelyn Preer, Dick Abrams, Lawrence Chenault and L. De-Bulger.(Bogle 32)

THE DUNGEON, a seven-reel feature, was produced by Oscar Micheaux in 1922. The Chicago Defender openly criticized Micheaux for using light-skinned actors and not advertising the film as a "Race" production.

Micheaux produced two versions of the film *BIRTHRIGHT*, the first a silent picture in 1924 featuring Evelyn Preer, J. Homer Tutt, Salem Tutt Whitney and Lawrence Chenault. The second version was a sound picture released in 1939 and featured Ethel Moses, Alec Lovejoy, and Carmen Newsom.

Micheaux was married in 1929 to Alice Russel, an actress who appeared in a number of his films and had a leading role in *GOD'S STEP CHILDREN*. The couple set up a home in Montclair, New Jersey, but both Micheaux and his wife did a lot of traveling around the country in the interest of the company. Although not an official member of the company, Mrs. Micheaux took charge of the office after Swan left the company.

Micheaux operated the company with a limited staff, primarily as an economy measure. He did all of the work himself. He wrote scenarios, supervised filming and did the bookkeeping; in short, he did everything. Micheaux Pictures took about an average of ten days to shoot and cost from $10,000 to $20,000. Micheaux usually obtained his actors from around the New York City area, frequently using actors of the Lafayette Players Stock Company. However, in several instances when filming on location he employed local talent. For example,

THE HOUSE BEHIND THE CEDARS, written by Charles W. Chestnutt, was filmed on location in Roanoke, Virginia. In this film he made generous use of local talent as extras. One of the familiar persons used was William "Big Bill" Crowell, who was at the time a popular fraternal leader in the state of Virginia. Other cast members included Shingzie Howard, Lawrence Chenault and Douglass Griffin. (Gehr 34)

Evelyn Preer, a member of the Lafayette Players Stock Company, was featured in many Micheaux films, as were Mercedes Gilbert, and Julia Theresa Russell, a sister-in-law of Micheaux.

Micheaux produced and directed *A DAUGHTER OF THE CONGO* in 1930 and his first "all-talkie" film, *THE EXILE*, in 1931. The cast which Micheaux assembled for *THE EXILE* included Charles Moore, Eunice Brooks, George Randol, Lorenzo Tucker, Nora Newsom, Stanley Morell, Inez Persaud, A.B. Comethiere, Norman Reeves, Lou Vernon, Carl Mahon, and a number of singers and dancers from "Blackbirds," "Brown Buddies," Connie's Inn, and the Cotton Club appeared in cabaret scenes in the picture. Both pictures met with some negative reaction. Micheaux was accused of perpetuating the "high yaller fetish" in *A DAUGHTER OF THE CONGO*. (Gehr 35)

THE EXILE had a successful premiere in New York City, but the first showing in Pittsburgh was halted mid-way through the showing. The action was taken by two members of the Pennsylvania Board of Censors, both women. Their reason for stopping the showing was that it did not carry the seal indicating that it had been passed by the State Censor Board. There was some speculation at the time, however, that the real reason for stopping the picture was that it contained scenes showing a Negro making love to a "near-white" woman. In a scene near the end of the picture (which the Censor Board members did not see) it is revealed that the woman actually had one percent "Negro" blood. Another scene in the picture shows a white man trying to take advantage of the woman and being soundly thrashed by the Negro who comes to her rescue. It was at this point that the picture was stopped. The background of *THE EXILE* is Chicago, at a time when blacks migrating from the south were pushing wealthy white property owners off South Parkway.

Micheaux produced two pictures in 1936, *TEMPTATION* and *UNDERWORLD*. Each picture cost about $15,000 to produce, of which approximately $2,000 was allocated for salaries to the actors. The minor actors were paid about $10 per day and the principals received from $100 to $500 per picture. All of the money, including production costs, was paid before the pictures were completed. For these two pictures, Micheaux used professional singers and dancers instead of trained dramatic actors. Most of the performers were nightclub stars instead of stage artists because, Micheaux claimed, he could depend on the former being available in one city at least until the picture was completed. Micheaux also stated that the big problem was getting the artists to work on time in the morning. This was a serious matter because the technicians, who were paid by the hour, would be standing around waiting for the performers to appear. (Gehr 36)

The picture *GOD'S STEPCHILDREN*, released in 1938, was probably the most notable of Micheaux's productions. The film was unique in that most of the important scenes were shot in a friend's home in front of a staircase where Micheaux found optimum lighting conditions.

GOD'S STEPCHILDREN had its world premiere at the RKO Regent Theatre, 116th Street, New York City; it was withdrawn after a two-day run and was later prohibited from being shown at any RKO Theatre in the country. The announcement of the ban followed previous announcements, made prior to each showing by Oscar Micheaux, that the objectionable parts of the picture had been deleted.

One scene which caused many of the patrons to get up and walk out of the theatre showed an actor, playing the part of white man, knocking down a young girl and spitting upon her because she had revealed that she had "colored blood" in her veins. Among those groups protesting the picture were the Young Communist League and the Nation Negro Congress. A clipping from a New York City newspaper reads, "the picture creates a false splitting of Negroes into light and dark groups. It slandered Negroes, holding them up to ridicule." (Gehr 37)

In 1940, Micheaux produced the *NOTORIOUS ELINOR LEE*, and announced that Negro aviator Col. Hubert Julian ("The Black Eagle") was joining the company as co-producer. The film had its world premiere in Harlem, complete with gold-engraved invitations, floodlights, a carpeted sidewalk, police, and Col, Julian as master of ceremonies in formal dress, top hat, white silk gloves and flowing cape.

Not much is known about the activities of the company after the release of *THE NOTORIOUS ELINOR LEE* in 1940. The last known activity of Micheaux was in 1948 when he wrote and directed the film *THE BETRAYAL* for Astor Pictures. The film was based on Micheaux's book, *The Wind from Nowhere.* Other books by Micheaux include, *The Case of Mrs. Wingate, The Masquerade, The Story of Dorothy Stanfield,* and The Forged Note.

Oscar Micheaux's most interesting contribution has often been viewed by some contemporary black audiences as his severest shortcoming. That his films reflected the interests and outlooks, the values and virtues, of the black bourgeoisie has long been held against him. Though his films rarely centered on the ghetto, few race movies did. They seldom dealt with racial misery or decay. Instead, Micheaux in his later films concentrated on problems facing black "professional people." Then, too, his leading performers-as was typical of race films-were often close to the white ideal; straight hair, keen features, light skin. However, Micheaux did not only have light-skinned actors and actresses in his films, he went for talent in acting and speech no matter what color; this is evident as Micheaux used Paul Robeson for the lead in *Body and Soul*, (1924)

Micheaux also had great vision for blacks in Hollywood, Micheaux did not like to see blacks always on the screen as uncle tom's and mammies. Micheaux hoped to create a star system like that of Hollywood: thus, Lorenzo Tucker was his Black Valentino; Ethel Moses was considered a Black Harlow; and Bee Freeman, a Black Mae West. To appreciate Micheaux's films one must understand that he was moving as far as possible from Hollywood's jesters and servants. He wanted to give his audience something to further the race, not hinder it. Often he sacrificed plausibility to do so. He created on occasion a deluxe, ideal world where blacks were just as affluent, just as educated, just as "cultured" as their white counterparts. Micheaux's shrewd promotional sense kept him in business, enabling him to produce, direct and write about 30 films from around 1919 to 1948. (Gehr 38)

Oscar Micheaux died in Charlotte, North Carolina in 1951 at the age of 67.

PROTEST, BURKEIAN ANALYSIS

Movies mirrored an American society that was strongly divided. One group of Americans, African Americans, were portrayed only through the eyes of the white majority, and thus left out of defining themselves in the fledgling motion picture industry.

Oscar Micheaux, an African American film pioneer, reacted to the need for an industry that served the African American community, and that would remedy the negative stereotypes of African Americans portrayed in motion pictures. (Bernstein 46)

His impact on the film industry was monumental, and yet remains virtually anonymous today. The power and mystery of the new technology mesmerized the public; images on the screen were often assumed to be the truth, including inaccurate representations of races. In response, a group of African American independent filmmakers, including Oscar Micheaux, tried to "uplift the race" and create unity within the black community. As this era unfolded, as early movies hardened the stereotypical lines between racial groups, Micheaux first personally overcame this, and then used the medium of the motion picture to communicate his ideas, and to portray African Americans with dignity and respect. In an article, "Dramatism as Ontology or Epistemology: A Symposium," Burke argues, "If people really do act in particular situations with certain purposes, then dramatism becomes the basic form from which one builds a theory of analysis about what is happening." (Burke 24) In recognizing how powerful film was, his impact was felt in the African American community, white community, and in the motion picture industry. Micheaux did not just direct films; he directed society away from resolute divisions.

An authentic representation of the African American experience was nonexistent. (Jones, 6) In early films, the black man was portrayed as subservient and happy-go-lucky. White actors had been imitating blacks since the first minstrel shows in 1840, and even before then in monologues and dances. For over 75 years, whites played blacks in "black face" by putting on thick black makeup. Many whites in the North saw the stereotypes of African Americans in the movies, and believed them. In early films, blacks played jungle natives, such as when Selig hired Pullman porters in Chicago to play "authentic" Africans in one of his most famous movies, *Big Game Hunting in Africa*. Many blacks also played comic buffoons or servile positions of maids and domestic help. (Bernstein 46)

In an effort to repudiate these stereotypes, African American entrepreneurs, eager to see an accurate reflection of their race on the screen, began to produce their own films. These were known as "race movies" and were often low-budget and technically inadequate. Yet African American moviemakers took on complex issues of the black community, including racial prejudice, poverty, and light versus dark skin. (Bernstein 46) African American studios appeared around the nation, in cities such as Los Angeles, Philadelphia, and Lincoln, Nebraska, but Chicago became the center for enterprising independent black filmmakers. Kenneth Burke attested, "symbols are actions which create potentialities, symbol-using is a creative activity which generates motive and potentiality." (Dramatism 448)

Jazz acts and vaudeville performers passed through Chicago, creating a mixed talent pool. (Bernstein 47) The initiation of black cinema was a tool of unification for the black community. Ossie Davis, a noted African American film actor stated, "There were black people behind the scenes, telling our black story to us as we sat in black theaters. Controlled by us, created by us-our own image, as we saw ourselves..." (Jones 6)

One of the most influential African American filmmakers to establish himself in this period was Oscar Micheaux. Micheaux responded to the desire for unity within the black community as well as to the stereotypes in early films. He was the first African American man to produce films in both the silent and sound eras. (Sampson 10) Later in his life, he was the first filmmaker to use technology to invent certain film techniques that had never been seen before. Micheaux's mission is confirmed in this statement: "The appreciation my people have shown my maiden efforts convinces me that they want racial photoplays, depicting racial life, and to that task, I have consecrated my mind and efforts." (*The Chicago Defender*, 31 January 1920) In *A Rhetoric of Motives,* Burke contends, "identification is an "acting together" that grows out of the ambiguities of substance, to the extent that the actors share a locus of motives. To the extent the audiences accept and reject the same ideas, people, and institutions, that the speakers do, identification occurs." (Burke 21)

His success was truly miraculous-Micheaux overcame racial and financial difficulties in order to gain independence, stray from the stereotypes he was born into, and make remarkable changes in the film industry, African American community, and American society. Micheaux used the new technology to deliver a message. Themes he often focused on included African Americans passing for white, intermarriage, injustice of the courts against blacks and even the sensitive subjects of lynching and the Ku Klux Klan. (Jones 29) In *A Grammar of Motives*, Burke argues, "Identification often becomes so strong as to indicate the unity of the individual with some cosmic or universal purpose." (Burke 288)

Released just five months after the Chicago Race Riots and the "Red Summer of 1919," *Within Our Gates* contained a riot-lynching scene which reflected American race relations in the early part of the century. The film included a sequence depicting the lynching of two innocent African Americans, a woman and her sharecropper husband who was accused of murdering his employer, a white plantation owner. (Diawara 49) It was advertised in the *Chicago Defender* as "the greatest preachment against race prejudice." The *Defender* also stated that "it is the claim of the author and producer that, while it is a bit radical, it is the biggest protest against Race prejudice, lynching and concubinage that was ever written or filmed. (17 January 1920, 12)

The attempt to ban screenings of Micheaux's film, then, was an attempt to silence the protest against lynching. *Within Our Gates* was thus historically linked to fear of cataclysmic social change, a linkage obfuscated by the smoke screen of race riots. "Micheaux's spectacle of lynching was rhetorically organized to encourage the feeling of righteous indignation in the Black spectator." (Diawara 50) The lynching of the man and wife in the film is a scene that is one of the most unsettling images in the history of African American cinema. (Diawara 55)

A triumph for Micheaux, *Within Our Gates* was a rejoinder against the prevalent racial stereotypes in movies and opened a new door of consideration for the African American community, but the white community as well; whites began to recognize the power of Micheaux and the challenge the African American community was making to racism.

In *A Grammar of Motives*, Burke uses Webster's dictionary to define substance, "the most important element."

5
CONCLUSIONS

The History of the Modern World was made in the main, by what was taken from African people. Europeans emerged from what they call their "Middle-Ages," people poor, land poor and resources poor; and to a great extent culture poor. They raided and raped the cultures of the world, mostly Africa, and filled their homes and museums with treasures, then they called the people primitive.

African-Americans are the least integrated and the most neglected of groups in the historical interpretation of the American experience. The neglect has made this study of Artists as Activists during the Harlem Renaissance an increasing necessity.

Egypt and the nations of the Nile Valley were, figuratively, the beating heart of Africa and the incubator for its greatness for more than a thousand years. Egypt gave birth to what later would become known as, "Western Civilization," long before the greatness of Greece and Rome. In the distance this is a part of the African-American story, such a polemic is presented in the various essays and pieces of fiction found during the Harlem Renaissance. Alain Locke's anthology, *The New Negro* published in 1925, is the manifesto of The New Negro Movement, of the Harlem Renaissance.

According to the *Webster's Ninth New Collegiate Dictionary*, identification means, "psychological orientation of the self in regard to something as a person or group with a resulting feeling of close emotional association: a largely unconscious process whereby an individual models thoughts, feelings, and actions after those attributed to an object that has been incorporated as a mental image." From this common identity, group members develop shared values and similar patterns of behavior. The primary linguistic forms of identification are the inclusive plural pronouns "we" and "you" and the exclusive "they".

The New Negro must then be defined as an early twentieth century African American man and/or woman who are painfully aware of historical oppression and unjust exclusion from American institutions. Harlem Renaissance Artists dealt with the Society's inability to welcome them graciously as competent, de-

serving members. Harlem Renaissance Artists possessed an enlightened understanding of their race and sought to educate their counterparts as to the evolution
of a new black aesthetic and political ideal in America. In *A Grammar of Motives*, Burke cogently argues, "The principle of substance is important in rhetorical criticism because all discourse must establish a substance that is the context
for the communication or the key to the speaker's attitude." (Burke 29)

With the publication of *The New Negro*, Locke became the leading theoreti-
cian and strategist of the New Negro Movement. Due to the publication of *The
New Negro*, critics were forced to take black writing seriously, and it served to
unite struggling black authors of that period. Locke was a self-confessed "philosophical midwife" to a generation of black artists and writers.

Kenneth Burke in his book, *Language As Symbolic Action*, argues, "termin-
istic screen of their rhetorical vision or their shared social reality. (Burke 141)

As Alain Locke laid down the "how to guide" or map of the New Negro
movement, W.E.B. DuBois was the leader/project manager of the Harlem Renaissance. DuBois had a way of creating solidarity between the artists and being
the interpreter of African American cultural ideology. Kenneth Burke in his
book, *Permanence and Change*, states, "Action and end and dramatistic terms
are appropriate in discussing human conduct" (Burke 276)

African Americans had entered an era of vitality and Harlem was the liveli-
est expression of this ebullience. Harlem was the headquarters of Marcus
Garvey and his Back-to-Africa movement, W. E.B.DuBois and the N.A.A.C.P.,
the *Messenger* magazine and the African American radical movement; it became
the hub of the Black cultural and intellectual world. Soon the community was
acknowledged as the "Black Metropolis" and its people the "New Negro."
Thus, Harlem was an attraction to African Americans everywhere, and they
surged into the area from city, town and village in the South, Africa and the
West Indies. The lure of Harlem was felt by every African American in the
world.

In any communication situation, a level of total understanding is truly important. It is obvious that Kenneth Burke is one of the most distinguished theo-
rist of language and rhetoric in our era. According to Burke in *A Rhetoric of
Motives*, 1950, people are divided from one another: there is overlap between
people: We share some experiences, values, language, and so forth. Burke
thinks communication is the primary was in which people transcend their divisions and enlarge what is common to them. Burke sees of building common
ground as a process of identification, or recognizing and enlarging commonal-
ities between each other.

Bracey, Meier and Rudwick in their book, *The Afro Americans: Selected
Documents*, Langston Hughes wrote, "When the Negro was in Vogue", he recalls, "The Saturday night rent parties that I attended were often more amusing
than any night club, in small apartments where God knows who lived-because
the guests seldom did-but where the piano would often be augmented by a guitar, or an odd cornet, or somebody with a pair of drums walking in off the street.

And where awful bootleg whiskey and good fried fish or steaming chitterling were sold at very low prices." (Hughes 548)

Harlem was a city within a city, with its class divisions as well: poor people living in the "Valley" and the well-to-do on "Sugar Hill". The "Valley" contained the dance halls, cabarets, honkytonks, fish shacks, juck joints, hole-in-the-wall night clubs and the red light district. Few apartments were steam-heated; rents were low, whiskey cheap, fights frequent and unlicensed honkytonks kept one jump ahead of the law. Yet everywhere in Harlem there seemed to be gaiety, good feeling and the sound of jazz bands. People were dancing to the syncopations of Fletcher Henderson, listening to the Blues of Bessie Smith, and rocking to the trumpet of Louis "Satchmo" Armstrong (my home boy from New Orleans). Langston Hughes writes in "When the Negro was in Vogue", "the dancing and singing and impromptu entertaining went on until dawn came in at the windows. These parties, often termed whist parties or dances, were usually announced by brightly colored cards stuck in the grille of apartment house elevators, the cards were highly entertaining in themselves." (Hughes 548).

In *A Grammar of Motives*, Burke uses his pentad as a tool for understanding identification. These dramatistic terms are act, scene, agent(s), agency, purpose. (Burke 128).

The Harlem Renaissance created a New Negro Movement(Act). Harlem was the place of this lively artistic exchange(Scene). The Artists as Social Activists examined in this dissertation and others(Agents). The creation of African American artistic expression as a response to oppression(Agency). Liberation, freedom, justice, and equality for all African Americans(Purpose).

The Harlem Renaissance was a sudden awakening, a national sweep of literature, dance, music, theatre and film. Successful musical shows appeared on Broadway, which called attention to African American talent. The first production was Shuffle Along which ran nearly two years on Broadway. Four African Americans- Flournoy Miller, Aubrey Lyles, Noble Sissle and Eubie Blake- combined their talents to produce this musical which featured an unknown Josephine Baker.

James Weldon Johnson in his article, "The Negro Artist and his Reception", published by Gilbert Osofsky in his book, *The Burden of Race*, Johnson writes, "The trained Negro musician, the literary Negro poet, the legitimate Negro actor, and the skilled Negro artist are becoming more and more figures in the foreground of American culture." (Johnson 321)

As Robert Hayden attested in the preface of *The New Negro* by Alain Locke, "The Negro became a "vogue," partly as the result of a growing interest in his jazz, spirituals, and folklore, partly as the result of the glamour and notoriety brought to the Harlem Renaissance." (Hayden xi)

DuBois wrote an article in the *Atlantic Monthly* in 1901 which said, "The problem of the Twentieth Century is the problem of the color-line...modern democracy cannot succeed unless the peoples of different races and religions are also integrated into the democratic whole." (DuBois 369)   Will race be the greatest problem of the 21st. Century?

Wilson argued in *The Declining Significance of Race*, "the growing importance of class and the decreasing significance of race in determining blacks' chances in life." (Wilson 1978a)

Willie argued in *The Inclining Significance of Race*, his response to Wilson's analysis, for the inclining significance of race "especially for middle-class blacks who, because of school desegregation and affirmative action and other integration programs, are coming into direct contact with whites." (Willie 1978) In the minds of many scholars and intellectuals, the class-over-race debate appears to be one that is settled, and settled in fairly absolute terms. For a significant group of scholars in the field of race relations and within the discipline of sociology in general, as well as other disciplines, class, not race, is the determining factor for progress and successful mobility in contemporary U.S. society. For these scholars, virtually the only causal stratification variable of black achievement that is recognized is class.

Despite the well-structured, fact-based arguments of Willie and others who provide evidence that race persists as a powerful deterrent to black success across all class lines, this reality has not been grasped or admitted to by all. Wilson, the leading proponent of the class-over-race argument, has provided a basis for substantiating the claims of those who are no longer willing to admit to the pervasiveness of racism as a sickness that plagues our society.

Why the tendency for some to admit to class and not race? For some, it may be ignorance of the realities of the minority experience in the United States. For others, the class-over-race argument may be more palatable. Some may perceive class bias as a more palatable form of inequality-less insidious than race bias. Admitting the existence of a classist versus racist society may in some ways be less offensive to those who view themselves as progressive-minded Americans.

Although class certainly is a determinant of the opportunities afforded all Americans-black, white, and other-we cannot attribute the primary cause of limited black progress to class alone. Many blacks left at the superdome in New Orleans during hurricane Katrina would certainly not support the class-over-race argument. For them, the significance of race undeniably continues. In *Permanence and Change*, Burke purports, "Authority, in turn, establishes definite relationships among people, reflecting how much power they possess. These relationships can be viewed as a ladder of authority or the hierarchy of society." (Burke 276)

Although the initial formulations of these arguments were published several decades ago, the argument of both Wilson and Willie certainly had validity then and continue to do so now. Neither should or can be dismissed.

Kenneth Burke in his book, *Permanence and Change*, argues, "The sense of mystery that one class holds for another class and the upward tendencies of the lower classes create a guilt that is inherent in the hierarchy itself." (Burke 283)

DuBois argues in *The Souls of Black Folk,* that the Negro grows weary of constructed psychology that requires that he at once have two being in body in one soul, "After the Egyptian and Indian, the Greek and Roman, the Teuton and Mongolian, the Negro is a sort of seventh son, born with a veil, and gifted with a second-sight in this American world which yields him no true self consciousness, this sense of always looking at oneself through the eyes of others, of measuring one's soul by the tape of a world that looks on in amused contempt and pity." (DuBois 8) Here, DuBois makes one of the most psychoanalytical observations of the impact that racism, slavery and segregation has on the African American's ability to articulate mental and physical selfhood. Walking on this psychological tight rope was more than a balancing act. As DuBois explains, "one ever feels his twoness,-an American, a Negro; two souls, two thoughts two unreconciled strivings; two warring ideals in one dark body whose dogged strength alone keeps it from being torn asunder." (DuBois 8) In *The Rhetoric of Religion*, Burke presents all concepts as paired opposites a type of twoness, "good and evil, God and devil, bless and curse, order and disorder, obedience and disobedience and promise and threat." (Burke 184)

The African American writer Peter Abrahams writes that before reading *The Souls of Black Folk* by DuBois, "he had no words with which to voice his Negro-ness" as Saunders Redding explains in *Black Voices*, "without question, DuBois skillfully unravels and articulates with unwitting clairvoyance the Vers libre, psycho-dramatic shackles of a conflicted, inflicted and enforced exterior constructed self." Saunders further argues that it may be observed as "fixing that moment in history when the American Negro began to reject the idea that the world belong to white people only." (Redding vii) DuBois furthers this theory of psychological deconstruction: "Wizzard of the North-the Capitalist-and the new agent of the south conspired to shackle and control to maintain his own literature, music, art or dance, uses his craft during this epoch to free his or her people from the psycho sociological shackles that they played no role in crafting. At the same moment, aided in freeing the Euro-American from his self constructed psycho sociological shackles."(DuBois 122)

Thus, it is in this context that the researcher seeks to analyze what he terms the psychosociological movement, a conjoined effort, to liberate the whole of humanity. At this point in American history, we observe the African American beginning to analyze the Eurocentric psychic. For DuBois cogently argues: "The martyrdom of man may be increased and prolonged through primitive biological racial propaganda, but on the hand through cooperation, education and understanding cultural race unit may be the pipeline through which human civilization may extend to wider and wider areas to the fertilization of mankind." (DuBois 123)

The psychosociological interpretation of race now takes precedence and becomes firmly entrenched in the American mindset. Within the United States, one finds an evolving interpretation of race that is associated with DuBois and Kenneth Stamps terms America's "peculiar institution, slavery".

In the early part of the 20th century, scholars and rehtors such as W.E.B.DuBois called attention to White privilege and to the racism inherent in Whites' attitudes toward Blacks. Writing for the *Independent* in 1910, DuBois questions the "Souls of White Folk," arguing that even liberal philanthropic Whites desire Blacks to be subservient, humble, and thankful for the few charitable acts bestowed upon them. "But when the black man begins to dispute the white man's title to certain alleged bequests of the Father's in wage and position, authority and training; and when his attitude of charity is sullen anger rather than humble jollity; when he insists on his human right to swagger and swear and waste-then the spell is suddenly broken and the philanthropist is apt to be ready to believe that Negroes are impudent and that the South is right." (quoted in Lewis 470)

For DuBois, whiteness was "a two-hundred-year-old dogma of stupendous fraudulence that was well on the way to supplanting Christianity, humanity and democracy" (Lewis 13) He argues that the "conquering ideology of whiteness," is the "most pernicious invention" of the modern age (Lewis 96) Indeed, people of color have undertaken critical examinations of whiteness for centuries but it has only been in recent decades that studies of whiteness as a social and racial identity have gained popularity within most academic circles. The reasons for this renewed (or new) interest in whiteness should not go uninterrogated. In an academic climate in which subject position increasingly matters, with race and gender among the most overt indicators, it is possible that White scholars seek to reaffirm their claims on knowledge by participating in the dialogue on multiculturalism. A comparison can be made here between studies in whiteness and studies in masculinity. In both cases, the best research is aimed not at securing a space for dominant identities to assert their dominance yet again. Rather, it endeavors to find the fissures in those everyday practices of domination, the points of resistance and reconfiguration that might enable us to actively participate in the remaking of ourselves and our world. Leland Griffin in "The Rhetorical Structure of the New Left Movement." Quotes Burke's dramatistic scene—to a abroad rhetorical purpose; speaking of the March on Washington, he writes: "From the standpoint of rhetorical function, however, one might suggest that the March provided the "New Left" movement with a highly appropriate symbol: the symbol of solidarity—a massive symbol of people in movement—of people identify-ing in the name of freedom, justice and equality—of people committed, and acting in cooperation, hope, and above all, peace, for "a better world."(Griffin *QJS* 1964 50: 33)

I opt for a redesign of our views on race, class and culture; a world where race does not matter and is not the greatest problem of the 21st century; a redesign of the world, where we can find significant solidarity, tolerance, diversity, multiculturalism in a global village. I contend we can live in a global village without exclusion, vilification, marginalization, schematization; a world of rich semiotics and openness with only glorification of the masses, by the workers and for the peoples of this UNITED GLOBAL VILLAGE.

BIBLIOGRAPHY

AFRICAN AMERICAN ART AND CULTURE

Anderson, Marian. *My Lord, What A Morning*. New York: Avon, 1956.
Appiah, K. Anthony and Gutmann, Amy. *Color Conscious: The Political Morality of Race*. Princeton, NJ: Princeton University Press, 1996.
Baldwin, James. *The Fire Next Time*. New York: Dial, 1963.
Barksdale, Richard K. *Praisesong of Survival*. Urbana: University of Illinois Press, 1992.
Bell, Derrick. *Faces At The Bottom of the Well: The Permanence of Racism*. New York: Basic Books, 1992.
Bassett, John Earl. *Harlem in Review: Critical Reactions to Black American Writers*. London: Associated University Presses, 1992.
Beckford, Ruth. *Katherine Dunham, A Biography*.
New York: Dekker, 1979.
Berry, Faith. *Langston Hughes, Before and Beyond Harlem*. New York: Wing Books, 1995.
Bigsby, C.W. *The Black American Writer: Poetry and Drama*. Baltimore: Penguin, 1971.
Bogle, Donald. *Blacks In American Film and Television*. New York: Garland, 1988.
Bogle, Donald. *Toms, Coons, Mulatooes, Mammies, and Bucks; An Interpretive History of Blacks in American Film*. New York: Viking, 1973.
Bontemps, Arna, ed. *American Negro Poetry*. New York: Hill & Wang, 1963.
Bracey,J., Meier,A., Rudwick,E. *The Afro-Americans: Selected Documents*. Boston: Allyn & Bacon, 1972.
Bradley, David and Fishkin, Shelley F.,eds. *The Encyclopedia of Civil Rights in America*. Armonk, NY: Sharpe Reference, 1998.
Braithwaite, W.S. *The Poetic Year for 1916, A Critical Anthology*. Boston:

Small, Maynard, 1917.

Brawley, Benjamin G. *The Negro in Literature and Art in the United States.* New York: Dodd, Mead & Company, 1934.

Brisbane, Robert. *The Black Vanguard.* Valley Forge,PA.: Judson, 1970.

Bronz, Stephen. *The Roots of Negro Racial Consciousness-The 1920s: Three Harlem Renaissance Authors.* New York: Libra, 1964.

Brown,S., Davis,A., Lee,U. *The Negro Caravan.* New York: Arno, 1970.

Butcher, Margaret Just. *The Negro in American Culture.* New York: Alfred A. Knopf, 1956.

Calverton, V.F.ed. *Anthology of American Negro Literature.* New York: The Modern Library, 1929.

Candaele, Kerry. *Bound for Glory, 1910-1930: From the Great Migration to The Harlem Renaissance.* New York: Chelsea House, 1997.

Chambers, Veronica. *The Harlem Renaissance.* Philadelphia: Chelsea House, 1998.

Clayton, Obie, Jr.,ed. *An American Dilemma Revisited: Race Relations in a Changing World.* New York: Russell Sage Foundation, 1996.

Coleman, Jonathan. *Long Way to Go: Black and White in America.* New York: Atlantic Monthly Press, 1997.

Cose, Ellis. *Color-Blind: Seeing Beyond Race in a Race-Obsessed World.* New York: Harper Collins, 1997.

Davis, A.P. *From the Dark Tower; Afro-American Writers 1900-1960.* Washington,D.C.: Howard University, 1974.

Diawara, Manthia. *Black American Cinema.* New York: Routledge, 1993.

Diawara, Manthia. *Black Cinema.* Baltimore: Johns Hopkins University, 1991.

Dillard, J.L. *Black English Its History and Usage in the United States.* New York: Vintage, 1972.

Dover, Cedric. *American Negro Artist.* Bombay: Asia House, 1960.

Duberman, Martin. *Paul Robeson.* New York: Knopf, 1989.

Dunham, Katherine. *Island Possessed.* Garden City, New York: Doubleday, 1969.

DuBois, W.E.B. *The Autobiography of W.E.B.DuBois: A Soliloquy On Viewing My Life From The Last Decade Of Its First Century.* New York: International, 1968.

DuBois, W.E.B. *The Suppression of the African Slave-Trade to the United States of America 1638-1870.* New York: Longmans, 1896.

Edelstein, T., Scheiner, S. *The Black Americans-Interpretative Readings.* New York: Holt, 1971.

Edwards, Lee. *Psyche As Hero: Female Heroism and Fictional Form.* Middletown,CT.: Wesleyan, 1984.

Fauset, Jessie. *There is Confusion.* New York: Boni & Liveright, 1924.

Feeney, Joseph. "Jessie Fauset of the Crisis: Novelist, Feminist, Centenarian," *Crisis.* 90: 1983.

Franklin, John Hope and Moss, Alfred A., Jr. *From Slavery to Freedom: A His-*

tory of African Americans. Seventh ed. New York: Knopf, 1994.

Gates, Henry Louis, Jr. and West, Cornel. *The Future of the Race*. New York: Knopf, 1996.

Gehr, Richard. "One Man Show," *American Film*. 16: 1991.

Gewen, Barryl. "The Robeson Record," *The New Leader*. 72: 1989.

Gloster, Hugh. *Negro Voices In American Fiction*. New York: Russell, 1965.

Hacker, Andrew. *Two Nations: Black and White, Separate, Hostile, Unequal*. New York: Scribners, 1992.

Hughes, Langston. *The Big Sea*. New York: Hill & Wang, 1940.

Johnson, James W. *Along This Way*. New York: Viking, 1933.

Johnson, James W. *Negro Americans, What Now?*. New York: Viking, 1934.

Johnson, James W. *The Book of American Negro Poetry*. New York: Harcourt, 1922.

Kennedy, Randall. *Race, Crime and the Law*. New York: Pantheon, 1997.

Kesteloot, Lilyan. *Anthologie Negro-Africaine Panaroma Critique Des Prosateurs, Poetes Et Ddramaturges Noirs*. Paris: Edicef, 1992.

Layton, William. "A Paul Robeson Retrospectie," *Freedomways*. 25: 1985.

Lewis, V.C. "Mulatto Hegemony in the Novels of Jessie Redmon Fauset," *CLA Journal*. 35: 1992.

Locke, Alain. *The New Negro*. New York: Atheneum, 1975.

Maynard, Richard. *The Blackman On Film: Racial Stereotyping*. Rochelle Park,N.J.: Hayden, 1974.

Meiers, August. *Negro Thought In America*. Ann Arbor: University of Michigan, 1968.

Murray, Hugh. "Paul Robeson: A Perspective," *Journal of Ethnic Studies*. 18: 1990.

Myrdal, Gunnar et al. *An American Dilemma: The Negro Problem and Modern Democracy*. New York: Harper, 1944.

Newman, Shirlee. *Marian Anderson: Lady From Philadelphia*. Philadelphia: Westminister, 1966.

Norment, Lynn. "Directors Guild Honors Filmaker Oscar Micheaux," *Jet* 70: 1986.

Osofsky, Gilbert. *The Burden of Race*. New York: Harper & Row, 1967.

Ottley, Roi. *Black Odyssey*. New York: Scribner's, 1948.

Powell, A.C. jr. *Marching Blacks*. New York: Dial, 1945.

Patterson, Orlando. *The Ordeal of Integration: Progress and Resentment in America's "Racial" Crisis*. Washington, DC: Civitas/Counterpoint, 1998.

Quarles, Benjamin. *The Negro in the Making of America*. New York: Collier, 1964.

Quarles,B., Fishel,L. *The Negro American A Documentary History*. Glenview, Ill.: Scott, Foresman, 1967.

Robeson, Paul. *Here I Stand*. New York: Dobson, 1958.

Robeson, Paul. *Paul Robeson Speaks: Writings, Speeches, Interviews, 1918-*

1974. New York: Brunner/Mazel, 1978.

Sarat, Austin, ed., *Race, Law, and Culture: Reflections on Brown v. Board of Education*. New York: Oxford, 1997.

Shipler, David K. *A Country of Strangers: Black and White in America*. New York: Knopf, 1997

Sigler, Jay A. *Civil Rights in America: 1500 to the Present*. Detroit: Gale, 1998.

Sleeper, Jim. *Liberal Racism*. New York: Viking, 1997.

Steele, Shelby. *A Dream Deferred: The Second Betrayal of Black Freedom in America*. New York: Harper Collins, 1998.

Stevenson, Janet. *Marian Anderson: Singing to the World*. Chicago: Britannica, 1963.

Sylvander, C.W. *Jessie Redmon Fauset: Black American Writer*. Tron, N.Y.: Whitston, 1981.

West, Cornel. *Keeping Faith: Philosophy and Race in America*. New York: Routledge, 1993.

West, Cornel. *Race Matters*. Boston, Beacon Press, 1993.

CRITICAL AND CULTURAL THEORY

Arno, Theodor W. *Aesthetic Theory*. New York: Routledge & Kegan Paul, 1986.

Bell, Daniel. *The End of Ideology*. Glencoe, IL: The Free Press, 1960.

Benjamin, Walter. "Theses on the Philosophy of History." In *Illuminations*. New York: Schocken Books, 1969.

Boudon, Raymond. *The Analysis of Ideology*. Chicago: University of Chicago Press, 1989.

Bronner, Stephen Eric, and Douglas MacKay Kellner.(Eds.) *Critical Theory and Society: A Reader*. New York: Routledge, Chapman and Hall, 1989.

Calhoun, Craig.(Ed.) *Habermas and the Public Sphere*. Cambrtidge, MA: MIT Press, 1992.

Coward, Rosalind, and John Ellis. *Language and Materialism: Developments in Semiology and the Theory of the Subject*. London: Routledge & Kegan Paul, 1977.

Derrida, Jacques. *Writing and Difference*. Chicago: University of Chicago Press, 1978.

Eagleton, Terry. *Ideology: An Introduction*. New York: Verso, 1991.

Foucault, Michel. *The Archaeology of Knowledge*. New York: Harper & Row, 1976.

Fraser, Nancy. *Unruly Practices: Power, Discourse and Gender in Contemporary Social Theory*. Minneapolis: University of Minnesota Press, 1989.

Fukuyama, Francis. *The End of History and the Last Man*. New York: Free Press, 1992.

Grumley, John E. *History and Totality: Radical Historicism from Hegel to Fou-*

cault. New York: Routledge, 1989.

Habermas, Jurgen. *Moral Consciousness and Communicative Action.* Cambridge, MA: MIT Press, 1990.

Honneth, Axel. *The Critique of Power: Reflective Stages in a Critical Social Theory.* Cambridge, MA: MIT Press, 1991.

Lukacs, Georg. *History and Class Consciousness.* Cambridge, MA: MIT Press, 1971.

Marcuse, Herbert. *Counterrevolution and Revolt.* Boston: Beacon Press, 1972.

Marx, Karl. *Capital.* Vol.1. New York: International Publishers, 1967.

Meszaros, Istvan. *The Power of Ideology.* New York: New York University Press, 1989.

Nelson, Gary, and Lawrence Grossberg. (Eds.) *Marxism and the Interpretation of Culture.* Chicago: University of Illinois Press, 1988.

Plamenatz, John. *Ideology.* New York: Praeger, 1970.

Ryan, Michael. *Marxism and Deconstruction: A Critical Articulation.* Baltimore: Johns Hopkins University Press, 1982.

Spivak, Gayatri. *In Other Worlds: Essays in Cultural Politics.* New York: Methuen, 1987.

Wellmer, Albrecht. "Communications and Emancipation: Reflections on the Linguistic Turn in Critical Theory." In *On Critical Theory.* Ed. John O'Neill. New York: Seabury Press, 1976.

RHETORICAL CRITICISM AND SOCIAL MOVEMENT RHETORIC

Brock, Bernard. *Kenneth Burke and Contemnporary European Thought: Rhetoric in Transition.* Tuscaloosa: U. of Alabama, 1995.

Brock, Bernard. *Kenneeth Burke and the 21st. Century.* Albany: State U. of New York, 1999.

Burke, Kenneth. *A Grammar of Motives.* Berkeley: University of California, 1945.

Burke, Kenneth. *A Rhetoric of Motives.* Berkeley: University of California, 1950.

Burke, Kenneth. *Attitudes Toward History.* Berkeley/Los Angeles: University of California Press, 1937.

Burke, Kenneth. *Language As Symbolic Action. Essays on Life, Literature and Method.* Berkeley/Los Angeles: University of California Press, 1966.

Burke, Kenneth. *On Symbols and Society.* Ed. Joseph R. Gusfield. Chicago: University of Chicago Press, 1989.

Burke, Kenneth. *The Philosophy of Literary Form: Studies in Symbolic Action.* Berkeley/Los Angeles: University of California Press, 1941.

Burgchardt, Carl R. (Ed.) *Readings In Rhetorical Criticism.* 2nd edition. New York: Strata Publishing, 2000.

Carpenter, Ronald. *History as Rhetoric: Style, Narrative, and Persuasion.* Columbia: University of South Carolina Press, 1995.

Chesebro, James. *Extensions of the Burkeian System*. Tuscaloosa: Univ. of Alabama, 1993.

Clark, E.Culpepper. *The Schoolhouse Door: Segregation's Last Stand at the University of Alabama*. London: Oxford Press, 1993.

Eddy, Beth. *The Rites of Identity, Kenneth Burke & Ralph Ellison*. New Jersey: Princeton, 2003.

Goldzwig, Steven. *In a Perilous Hour: The Public Address of John F. Kennedy*. Greenwood Press, 1995.

Hammerback, John C. *A War of Words: Chicano Protest in the 1960s and 1970s*. Greenwood Press, 1985.

Jensen, Richard. *The Rhetoric of Agitation and Control*. Texas A&M Press, 1998.

Langer, Susanne. *Philosophy In A New Key: A Study In The Symbolism Of Reason, Rite and Art*. Cambridge,Mass.: Harvard University Press, 1957.

Moran, M.,Ballif, M. *Twentieth-Century Rhetorics and Rhetoricians*. Westport,CT.: Greenwood, 2000.

Olsen, Gregory. *Mansfield and Vietnam: A Study in Rhetorical Adaptation*. East Lansing: Michigan State U.Press, 1995.

Turner, Kathleen.(Ed.) *Doing Rhetorical History, Concepts and Cases*. Tuscaloosa: University of Alabama Press, 1998.

Young, Marilyn. *Flights of Fancy, Flight of Doom: KAL 007 and Soviet-American Rhetoric*. Lanham: University Press of America, 1988.

Zarefsky, David. Lincoln, Douglas, and Slavery: In the Crucible of Public Debate. Chicago: University of Chicago Press, 1990.

BIOGRAPHICAL SKETCH

Gregory Anthony Tillman, was born on April 14, 1956 in New Orleans, Louisiana, to Wilbert Leon Tillman and Theresa Hampton Tillman. The St. Monica Catholic School is where I matriculated as a young student, receiving a strong educational background in music, theatre and the performing arts, from the Sisters of the Blessed Sacrament. Interested in gospel music, I developed a strong passion and a love for gospel music and the arts, which lead me to become one of the "Original Gospel Soul Children of New Orleans". I received vocal and musical training from the late Albert Sylvester Hadley. I graduated from McDonogh #35 Senior High School in New Orleans, while a student at 35 (as it is called) I enjoyed speech and dramatic arts. My senior year I took 1st. in the City of New Orleans, 4th in the State of Louisiana and 6th in the Nation in oral interpretation of literature(Poetry and Prose). I took the B.A. in Political Science from Morehouse College in Atlanta, Georgia and the M.Ed. in Mass Communication from Southern University in Baton Rouge, Louisiana. At Morehouse College I was a member of the Morehouse College Glee Club, Speech and Debate Team, winner of the Benjamin E. Mays Debating Prize and received national finalist ranks from the National Forensic Association (3rd,4th & 7th., In the nation, in oral interpretation of literature, poetry; quarterfinalist, prose). After graduating Morehouse College, I began a career as a teacher of English and director of speech and debating. I am a member of the National Communication Association, National Forensic Association, National Association of Dramatic and Speech Arts, National Catholic Forensic League, and the Collegiate Forensic Association. I present conference papers and travel students to participate in intercollegiate forensics activities.